Everything You Ever Wanted To Know About Ghosts But Were Afraid To Ask!

Back cover photograph
The Tulip Staircase, Queen's House, Greenwich, England
Reverend W. C. Hardy
Courtesy of Mary Evans Picture Library/Peter Underwood

Everything You Ever Wanted To Know About Ghosts But Were Afraid To Ask!

Mark Lyon

Windwhistle Press

First Edition

ISBN 979-8-9871322-0-3

To those open-minded souls willing to accept the possibility of that which cannot, yet, be scientifically proven or, so far, fully explained, this book is enthusiastically dedicated.

Also available from Windwhistle Press

The Grey Ghost Book
By Jessie Adelaide Middleton

Another Grey Ghost Book
By Jessie Adelaide Middleton

The White Ghost Book
By Jessie Adelaide Middleton

Leap Castle
The House of Horrors
The Most Haunted Castle in Ireland
By Mildred Darby
Historical Introduction by Mark Lyon

San Francisco Ghosts
By Mark Lyon

Haunted Nevada City and Grass Valley
By Mark Lyon

Preface

So rang the words of an ancient Scottish prayer. Today, however, many of us no longer believe in such things. They consider the mere idea ghosts to be nothing more than an irrational and outdated remnant of the superstitions and fantastical beliefs of a bygone era.

But just how reasonable is an attitude which refuses to examine and seriously consider ideas and concepts which seem to fly in the face of reason and defy modern rationality?

It is often said that extraordinary claims require extraordinary proof. But is that really true? Who can say what exactly an extraordinary claim is and who is qualified to judge what sufficient proof is? The gorilla, the giant squid and the panda were all once thought to be mythical creatures and those who brought back reports of having seen them were laughed at by the scientists of their time. Instead of scoffing at that which cannot, yet, be demonstrated through extraordinary proof, I would suggest that wisdom requires the acceptance of at least the possibility of that which cannot, so far, be proven.

I am often asked, "Do you really believe in the existence of ghosts?" And to that I always answer, "No, I do not believe in the existence of ghosts. I know they exist." There is far too much evidence to believe otherwise."

Of course, many ghosts and "hauntings" may, upon investigation, be explained away as the misinterpretation of natural phenomena or as the result of a hallucination or conscious fraud. But it is impossible to dismiss the hundreds of carefully authenticated cases in which two or more credible and unrelated witnesses have described observing exactly the same apparition or have experienced exactly the same "ghostly" phenomenon in the same place without being aware of the other witness' experience. As the prolific writer and collector of true ghost stories, Harry Ludlum, put it, "Anyone stoutly maintaining that there are no such things is like a soldier on the battlefield denying the existence of bullets when they are flying all around him."

However, when we ask the question, "What is a ghost?" the subject becomes much more complicated. Many conflicting theories have been advanced over the years and a great deal of controversy has ensued.

While many believe that authentic encounters with ghosts provide incontrovertible proof of the survival of human consciousness past the death of the physical body, some parapsychologists, those who study such phenomena scientifically, feel that ghosts are merely echoes of the past, psychic imprints replaying themselves over and over again, unnoticed by all but those who are blessed, or should I say cursed, with the ability to see or hear them.

After studying accounts of ghostly encounters throughout my life, I have come to the conclusion that no one theory can adequately explain every case of what, for lack of a better term, we refer to as "ghosts."

As proof of the existence of ghosts and other supernatural entities relies entirely upon the testimony of those who claim to have encountered them, I have, whenever possible in the following pages, let the witnesses speak for themselves in their own words. While I, personally feel that all of the experiences recounted herein are true, it is up to the reader to judge for him or herself the veracity of each account.

With that in mind, I invite you to join me in an exploration of what appear to be true paranormal experiences and to, perhaps, consider employing proven techniques with which you, yourself, might investigate hauntings to be found in your own hometown. That being said, let us begin our journey into the extraordinary and mysterious world of ghosts.

Mark Lyon

Contents

My Own Personal Ghostly Encounters

The Haunted Apartment

Although I had been studying the subject of ghosts and other parapsychological phenomena throughout my life, it was not until I was twenty that I experienced my first ghostly encounter. While I was away from home, pursuing my baccalaureate degree at the University of San Francisco, my parents bought and moved into a house in Fresno, California. Built in 1945, the house featured a large and comfortable apartment built over and alongside the garage. While my parents and sister occupied bedrooms inside the house proper, my high school age brother and I were assigned to the apartment over the garage.

While, at first, my brother and I were delighted with this arrangement, when I arrived at the house for the first time at the conclusion of the school year, I was surprised to find that my brother had been sleeping each night on a couch in the house. Although he professed to not believe in the existence of ghosts, he stoutly declared that there was a threatening, indefinable "something" inhabiting the apartment over the garage and he refused to sleep in the apartment alone.

From the moment I first mounted the steep apartment staircase leading up to a bedroom on one side and a large sitting room on the other side, I felt the disquieting, unseen presence as well. There was the unmistakable feeling of continually being watched by a menacing "something" which was clearly objecting to our presence.

Still, I was determined to not be driven away by whatever was haunting the apartment and, although the feeling of being watched continued unabated, I slept in the apartment whenever I came home on school breaks and for several months following my graduation from university. During this time, I often heard a loud "bang" emanating from the bedroom door late at night, as if someone had fallen against it, followed by the distinct sound of what could only be described as a body falling down the staircase.

Finally, one day, I briefly but clearly saw the distinct form of a very young boy dressed in 1950's style blue jeans and a white t-shirt standing in the bedroom.

Although I will never know for certain why the apartment was haunted, a neighbor later told me a story which might, possibly, supply at least a partial explanation.

Many years before, the house had been owned by a physician who had lived there with his wife and young son. Then tragedy struck. The doctor's wife died and, while he was away at work, his son was left in the care of their housekeeper. Each afternoon the doctor would return to the house to have lunch with his son. One afternoon as he entered the driveway, the doctor was horrified to find his son hanging from the home's picket fence, the point of a picket firmly lodged into the boy's throat. While the doctor had arrived in time to save his son's life, the loss of oxygen to the boy's brain resulted in the boy becoming mentally retarded. Following this devastating event, the doctor sold the house and moved to another house in the same neighborhood.

By the time my parents had bought the house, the injured boy had grown to adulthood and I was told that he was often seen riding a bicycle through the neighborhood. One day, I saw him for myself. He stopped for a few moments by the picket fence, stared at the fence and the house, a look of sorrow on his face, and he, then, rode away.

I have often wondered if the unfortunate man on the bicycle could have, from time to time, while remembering happier days, projected an image of his younger self into the apartment, accounting for what I saw there.

Of course, this would not explain the malevolent feeling of being watched whenever I was in the apartment or the mysterious sounds issuing from the staircase and the bedroom door. The sense of threat which I felt in that apartment was so severe that, decades later, I still experience a moment of dread whenever I think about the time I spent there.

The Whaley House

It was during my undergraduate years that I spent almost an entire day at the Whaley House in San Diego, California in the hope of observing one of the numerous ghosts said to haunt that historic house.

Built in 1857, by Thomas Whaley, the residence once served as the San Diego County courthouse and, today, a large part of the first floor has been restored to look as the courtroom might have appeared at that time.

As I had chosen an overcast winter's day for my visit, with the exception of the curator, June Reading, I had the house all to myself throughout the entire morning and, much to my disappointment, I had experienced nothing which could be attributed to ghosts.

I was standing in the courtroom behind one of two lengths of chain meant to prevent visitors from entering the area beyond the spectator's benches when a tourist entered into the courtroom and Mrs. Reading began regaling the visitor with a story about how, when one day she was telling a group of school children about a violent storm Thomas Whaley had experienced at sea, one of the two chains began to undulate back and forth in the manner of an ocean wave.

Annoyed that I had, so far, not experienced anything of a paranormal nature in the house, I thought to myself, "If there really is a ghost here, I wish it would do something like that for me." Within seconds the chain in front of me began to swing back and forth. While it was swinging, I placed my hands above and below the chain in order to see if there were any remotely controlled wires attached to it or anything else which could account for the chain's movement. I even took a photograph of the chain while it was moving in the vain hope of catching a ghost on film. After the chain stopped swinging, I jumped up and down on the floor to see if that could cause the chain to swing but it stubbornly remained motionless.

The Roscrea Castle Ghost

A more tangible and explainable personal encounter with an unseen force occurred in 2005 when I was performing my original one-man musical play, *On Yonder Hill: An Irish-American Love Story*, as a part of Ireland's Heritage Week in Roscrea Castle in the town of Roscrea, County Tipperary, Ireland.

Built in the thirteen century, the castle is steeped in history and I knew that performing my play involving Irish history there, with the hearth of the castle's massive fireplace serving as my stage, would be an experience I would never forget. Little did I know how true that prediction would turn out to be.

I rehearsed the show on the afternoon prior to my performance and everything went splendidly, including the playing of my prerecorded musical accompaniments on a CD player which had been provided by the staff at the castle.

The night of my performance I waited in my dressing room (the medieval toilet chamber) for my entrance music. When I did not hear the music begin at the appointed hour, I started to wonder whether there might be a problem. I waited a little longer. Still, I heard no entrance music. Finally, after about ten minutes, I decided I had best sneak out behind the audience to where the CD player operator was seated and enquire as to why the show was being delayed.

"I can't get the CD to play," the man told me. He tried pressing play several times and I could see that he was right. Although the CD player had functioned perfectly only hours before, it now refused to function at all. "I have a great CD player at home, only a couple of blocks away," the man suggested. "I'll go home and get it. "You tell stories to the audience until I get back.' So that was what I did.

When the soundman got back he plugged in his CD player. We put my CD into the player and it played perfectly. I announced to the crowd that we were now ready to proceed but, when he pressed play, again, nothing happened. "It must be your CD," he suggested.

Fortunately, I had a back-up CD. We put it into the player and it played perfectly. Again, I announced that we were now ready to start but, when the man pressed play, again, the machine refused to play.

I had performed this show many times before and I had never had the slightest problem with my CDs. But, at this point, I had no choice but to perform the play without an accompaniment, singing thirteen songs a capella. The audience seemed pleased with this decision and everything was going well until, in the middle of the show, I clearly saw a tall, dark shadow-like form rise up before me, standing in the middle of the audience. The figure moved a few feet to the left and, then, vanished. I did my best to continue my performance as if nothing had happened.

Later that night an official with Heritage Ireland who had not been able to attend the show asked me, "How did it go?"

When I told her what had happened, she gave a look of grave concern and, without missing a beat, exclaimed, "The ghost of Damer!"

John Damer was a wealthy Englishman who, in 1722, had bought the castle and the entire town of Roscrae as well. In 1728, he built an elegant Queen Anne style mansion on the castle grounds, prudently situating the house within the castle's protective exterior fortifications. As Damer was a member of the English Ascendency who, at that time, lorded over and subjugated the native Irish, it was easy for me to understand why, if his ghost had seen the rehearsal of my play, with its pro-Irish independence theme, earlier that day, he would have wanted to stop me from performing it that night in his castle, a goal he almost succeeded in accomplishing.

When I asked the official from Heritage Ireland to tell me more about the ghost, she immediately began to backtrack, denying that the castle was actually haunted.

However, when I mentioned my experience at the next castle in which I performed my play a few days later, the official there said, "Oh, everyone knows that Roscrea Castle is haunted. They just don't want to admit it for fear of scaring away the tourists!"

Sounds in the Night

My most recent encounter with unseen presences occurred in the historic Holbrooke Hotel in the Gold Rush era town of Grass Valley, California. In 2010 I was asked to appear in an episode of the television program, *My Ghost Story*, concerning an intriguing photograph which had been taken at the Holbrooke; a photograph which will be discussed in my chapter on alleged photographs of ghosts.

After filming my portion of the *My Ghost Story* episode in Los Angeles, I was asked to help the show's film crew shoot B-roll footage at the Holbrooke at a later date. As a heavy snowstorm was expected the night of the B-roll shoot and the storm was predicted to continue into the next day, I was offered a room for two nights in the hotel.

Although I had initially been told to expect the two-person film crew to arrive by noon, their flight was canceled due to the inclement weather and I was told that they would, instead, travel to Grass Valley by car and that I should expect them to arrive at the hotel around midnight. I was the only guest in the hotel that night and I decided to wait up for the crew in my room. Twice, in the middle of the night, I clearly heard the sound of a conversation somewhere nearby in the hotel's upstairs hallways.

Each time that I heard the voices I felt certain it was the film crew and I got out of bed and made my way down the hall to the rooms which they were to occupy in order to ask what time in the morning they wished to begin shooting. Each time I ventured out of my room, however, there was no one to be found anywhere in the entire second floor.

The film crew finally arrived the following afternoon and we quickly accomplished all of the required filming. As I had remained awake throughout the entire previous night, by 11:00 p.m. I was tired and I decided to go to bed while the film crew continued to film downstairs in the hope of capturing a ghost on film. I checked the clock as I finally crawled into bed. It was 11:30. No sooner had I noted the time than I heard the distinct sound of someone jumping up and down on old-fashioned bedsprings along with rhythmic shouting. This seemed odd as the mattress on my bed was quite new, as were, I later learned, all of the mattresses in the hotel and, upon bouncing up and down on the bed, myself, I was unable to reproduce the sound. Although I found myself speculating as to the source of the unusual sounds, I was far too tired to attempt an investigation and I promptly fell asleep.

The next morning, at breakfast, I met a party of four women who had spent the night in Room 18 at the other end of the hotel, they being the only other guests booked in the hotel that night other than the film crew and myself. When they learned why I was there, one of the ladies said, "We need to tell you what happened last night."

It was 11:30 that night when they heard the same strange sounds which I had heard. They knew it was 11:30 as their television was on and *The Tonight Show* had just begun. Curious, they cautiously emerged from their room and followed the sounds down the hallway until, by one of the ladies placing her ear to the door of the room at the end of the hallway, Room 15, they determined that the sounds of someone jumping up and down on a bed were coming from inside that room, an unoccupied room which had not been booked that night, a room with a particularly intriguing history.

Among the ghosts said to haunt the Holbrooke are ghost children who have frequently been heard running up and down the upstairs hallways laughing and giggling. The children, it has been reported, can sometimes be heard playing inside an unoccupied room, particularly Rooms 15, 16 and 17, jumping up and down on the bed.

And, years before, a guest staying in Room 15 had enquired the next morning as to whether there had been an earthquake during the night. Upon learning that there been no earthquake, he responded, "I don't want to even think about any other possible explanation. In the middle of the night my bed began to jump up and down off the floor!"

Ghosts Which Interact with the Living

We often think of ghosts as fleeting images of light or shadow or, at best, as murky, transparent figures. But sometimes a ghost may appear to be so substantial that one would never suspect that what is being observed is not a normal, living entity. And sometimes, such a ghost may actually interact with the living. Consider the case of W. H. Stone who sent the following statement to the scientifically oriented Cambridge University men who founded the highly respected Society for Psychical Research in London.

A Friend from the Past

"I think it was in 1854. At that time we were large leather factors, and hide and skin brokers in Hopstown. When I say we, my employers were in the above line of business, and I was manager of the latter department, in which we used a large amount of stationery, such as weekly catalogues, black leads, and memorandum books, etc., for our buyers and our own men.

"I was going along from our office, in rather a merry mood, to order from a stationer in P. Street a quantity of catalogues wanted for next Friday's sale ... it might be some six or eight days before the great St. Leger day. I generally had a pound or two on the 'Leger' and it was my intention, as soon as my little order was given for stationery, to see a friend about the horse I had backed.

"Crossing from left to right in P. Street, whom should I meet (or as I thought met) but an old customer, as he had been for some years, of my father's. My father was formerly a brewer, and he had supplied the party I had met with ale, as I said, for some years, and I used to collect the accounts from him along with others in the same line. He was a beerhouse-keeper, or as they were then called, a jerry-shopkeeper.

"I went up to him, called him by his right name, shook him by the left hand for he had no right, it having been cut off when he was a youth. He had a substitute for a hand in the shape of a hook, and he was, said he, very active with this hook when his services were required in turning anyone out of his house that was in any way refractory.

"He was what you might call a jolly, good, even-tempered sort of a man, and much respected by his customers, most of whom did a little betting in the racing line. He had a very red countrified sort of a face, and dressed quite in a country style, with felt hat, something after the present style of billy-cocks, with thick blue silk handkerchief and round white dots on it, his coat, a sort of chedle-swinger, and a gold watchguard passing round his neck and over his waistcoat; his clothing was all of good material and respectably made.

"The moment he saw me his face shone bright, and he seemed much pleased to meet me, and I may say I felt a similar pleasure towards him. Mind, this occurred in perfect daylight, no moonlight or darkness so essential an accompaniment to ghost stories. Many people were passing and repassing at the time. You may be sure I did not stand in the middle of the street for about seven minutes talking and shaking hands with myself; someone would have had a laugh at me had that been the case.

"I almost at once, after the stereotyped compliments of the day, launched into the state of the odds respecting the St. Leger, and into the merits and demerits of various horses. He supplied me with what information I required, and we each went our way.

"He was a man considered to be well posted up in such matters, had cool judgment and discrimination; in fact, he was one of those that would not be led away by what are called tips. I made a memorandum or two, shook his hand again, and passed on about my business, ordered my catalogues, etc.

"I came back sauntering along towards the office, not now intending to see the party I had previously intended to see. As I got to the same part of P. Street, on my way back, I suddenly stood still, my whole body shook, and for the moment I tried to reason with myself. The man I had been speaking to was dead some four years before!

"Could it be possible that he had been buried alive? This is horribly shocking to think about, but such things have taken place. Decomposition being the only certain indication of death, might he not have been prematurely buried? ... I certainly saw his funeral.

"As I stood in the street I tried to give utterance to my thoughts and feelings, but no, I felt a sort of dumbness, and fairly gasped for breath. I felt a cold shiver come over me, although the day was warm. The hair of my head seemed as if it would force my hat off. My very blood seemed to object to perform its duty.

"The question might be asked: Was I unwell? Had I been indulging too freely in stimulants? In both cases I answer, No! For at that time I was particularly moderate in the use of stimulants, or tobacco, and was enjoying the most robust health, such as I never enjoyed before or since, and had a constitution like a horse.

"Was I annoyed in my mind in any way? Not in the least.

"Was it really a vision of the departed? Let the reader judge for himself. I give it up.

"Had I been deceived in having met the man? No such thing.

"Then was it someone very like him? Nothing of the sort, for the very words that passed between us could come from no other lips but the man himself, substantial flesh and blood.

"Was it an optical delusion? For nothing is so deceptive as optical delusions. Certainly not. We sometimes believe we see what we do not see, but in this case it was nothing of the sort, nor could it be somebody like him. It was him!

"As I said before, he had but one hand, and his right hand was his left one, in a sense. I had business transactions with him for many years. He had entirely slipped out of my memory for a length of time. That he was in or out of existence it never occurred to me for one moment till now; and the thought never presented itself throughout the interval between my going and coming, and perhaps never would have done, had I not gone the same way back, by way of P. Street, and passed the identical spot.

"It may be asked, am I, or was I, superstitious? I say, No, emphatically.

"To conclude, and as I have several times said before, and as I again say, I gave a start, and said, 'Bless me! How can this be?' Not an optical delusion, not it. What then? Nothing but a slight mystery, and I was confident I could easily solve it.

"Never was I more mistaken, for from that day to this I still remain in profound ignorance as to what was the cause or meaning of what I saw."

In evaluating this case we can easily rule out the possibility of Stone having hallucinated the entire experience. Others passing by on the busy street must have seen the man as well; for, as Stone, himself, points out, if he had stood there on the street for seven minutes talking to himself and shaking hands with no one to be seen, a crowd of laughing onlookers would surely have gathered about him.

We can also rule out the possibility of his old friend having been buried alive and, somehow, having been later rescued. If such a thing had occurred in Stone's small town, he could not have escaped becoming aware of the event.

In the hope of verifying Stone's account, the psychologist and a founding member of the Society for Psychical Research, Edmund Gurney, contacted F. A. Whaite, a fine arts gallery owner, who vividly recalled Stone's reaction on the day he encountered the tavern keeper's ghost.

"He did name it to me and my parents the same day;" Mr. Whaite wrote back to Gurney, "and I believe it was the truth, for he was so excited about it at the time."

The Lady with the Tea

A more recent and even more baffling event of a similar nature occurred in 1980 when a construction worker named Reg Blake and a friend were repairing the roof of the small Saint Barnabas Church on the Isle of Wight off the southern coast of England. They were both up on the roof when a petit, elderly lady came by carrying a vintage style aluminum thermos bottle.

"Hello, up there!" the lady called out to them. "I thought you might like some tea. You don't need to come down. I shall leave it for you in the church. I live just a little ways from here and you can bring me back the flask when you're done with it.'

They thanked the lady, took down her address and, a while after she had left, they climbed down from the roof. They each poured themselves a cup from the thermos. The tea was "stone cold" and it tasted terrible to boot! It tasted so awful that they unceremoniously disposed of it.

When they finished their day's work, Reg's friend set off for the address the lady had given them to return the thermos. But, upon his arrival, there was no house to be seen, only an empty lot. However he could plainly see that a house had once stood upon the property.

The next day, when the churchwarden came by to check on how their work was progressing, they told him about the elderly lady.

"Where did she say she lived?" the churchwarden inquired.

Upon hearing the address he replied, "That was my predecessor. She died three years ago!"

Twelve years later the church was deconsecrated and turned into a fresh produce market. The Isle of Wight historian and author, Gay Baldwin, recorded Reg Blake's account in her book, *Most Haunted Island, Isle of Wight Ghosts, Book 6*. When she asked the owner of the market if he had been visited by the elderly lady with the old fashioned aluminum thermos, he answered, "No, but if she does come by, I won't be drinking her tea!"

Apparitions
at
the Moment of Death

It is comforting to note that the largest number of verifiable ghostly encounters involve the appearance of a friend or loved one at precisely the moment of that person's death or very shortly thereafter in order to communicate that they are at peace and survive in, what for lack of a better term, we might call "The Otherside." And it is rare in my experience, after presenting a talk on the subject of ghosts, that I am not approached by someone in the audience who graciously shares with me such an experience which had occurred either to themselves or to a close family member.

A Vow Written in Blood

One of the most famous instances of such an experience occurred to the Scottish statesman, Henry Lord Brougham, who would eventually become the

Lord Chancellor of Great Britain; an incident which involved an old school chum to whom he referred in his account only as "G."

As recounted in *The Life and Times of Henry Lord Brougham, Written by Himself*, and copied by Lord Brougham from an account which he had written in his journal at the time of the event, Lord Brougham was traveling in Sweden with friends on the 18th of December in 1799.

"We set out for Gothenburg, determining to make for Norway," Lord Brougham wrote. "About one in the morning, arriving at a decent inn, we decided to stop for the night. Tired with the cold of yesterday, I was glad to take advantage of a hot bath before I turned in, and here a most remarkable thing happened to me — so remarkable that I must tell the story from the beginning.

"After I left the High School, I went with G., my most intimate friend, to attend the classes in the University. We frequently in our walks discussed and speculated upon many grave subjects — among others, on the immortality of the soul, and on a future state. This question, and the possibility, I will not say of ghosts walking, but of the dead appearing to the living, were subjects of much speculation: and we actually committed the folly of drawing up an agreement, written with our blood, to the effect that whichever of us died the first should appear to the other, and thus solve any doubts we had entertained of the 'life after death.' After we had finished our classes at the college, G. went to India, having got an appointment there in the Civil Service. He seldom wrote to me, and after the lapse of a few years I had almost forgotten him; moreover, his family having little connection with Edinburgh, I seldom saw or heard anything of them, or of him through them, so that all his schoolboy intimacy had died out, and I had nearly forgotten his existence.

"I had taken, as I have said, a warm bath, and while lying in it and enjoying the comfort of the heat, after the late freezing I had undergone, I turned my head round, looking towards the chair on which I had deposited my clothes, as I was about to get out of the bath. On the chair sat G., looking calmly at me. How I got out of the bath I know not, but on recovering my senses I found myself sprawling on the floor. The apparition, or whatever it was, that had taken the likeness of G., had disappeared.

"This vision produced such a shock that I had no inclination to talk about it or to speak about it but the impression it made upon me was too vivid to be easily forgotten; and so strongly was I affected by it that I have here written down the whole history, with the date, 19th December, and all the particulars, as they are now fresh before me.

"I recollected quickly enough our old discussion and the bargain we had made. I could not discharge from my mind the impression that G. must have died, and that his appearance to me was to be received by me as a proof of a future state."

In October, 1862, Lord Brougham added this postscript to the story:

"And now to finish the story, begun about 60 years since. Soon after my return to Edinburgh, there arrived a letter from India, announcing G.'s death, and stating that he had died on the 19th of December!"

A Vision of Death

A much more common example of such an event was reported to the Society for Psychical Research.

"During my college days," wrote their informant, "I had a very dear and intimate chum, R. F. Dombrain. We used to walk together, read together, pray together, and would have thought it wrong to keep any secret from each other. We hoped to go together into the foreign mission-field but my friend was ready to go before I was, and it was while he was in London making arrangements about going abroad, that he was seized with a very bad fever, and his life for some time despaired of. At last he recovered and returned to Dublin, where I saw him several times.

He was not quite restored to health, but I hoped he would soon be so. This was the state of things when I went down to the County Limerick, in the spring of 1853. I received a few letters from my friend which told me of gradually improving health. I was busily occupied about my mission work at the village of Doon, and felt perfectly at ease about my dear friend's recovery.

"A few days had elapsed without any tidings reaching me, when on the morning of the 14th of April I had the most vivid dream I remember ever to have seen. I seemed to be walking with young Dombrain, amidst some beautiful scenery, when suddenly I was brought to a waking condition by a sort of light appearing before me. I started up in my bed, and saw before me, in his ordinary dress and appearance, my friend, who seemed to be passing from earth towards the light above. He seemed to give me one loving smile, and I felt that his look contained an expression of affectionate separation and farewell. Then I leaped out of bed, and cried with a loud voice, 'Robert, Robert,' and the vision was gone.

"In the house there was sleeping a young servant boy, whose name was also Robert. He came running into my room, saying that my loud cry had awakened him from sound sleep, and that he thought I was ill. The whole scene was so impressed upon my mind that I felt the death of my friend just as really as if I had been by his bedside, and seen him pass away. I had looked at my watch and found the time three minutes past five. I knew that at that moment my friend's spirit had passed from his body. I could think of nothing else. ... During the whole of the day the same sad gloom weighed down my mind which I should have felt had I been with my friend at his death-bed. I wrote to my sister asking for particulars and I wished to know the exact time the death had taken place. Never once did the slightest doubt cross my mind that my friend had died.

"The following morning I received a letter from my sister, stating that for a few days Mr. Dombrain had not been so well, and that at three minutes past five in the morning he had quietly passed away from this world. Since then I have very often mentioned the circumstance to friends, and the deep impression made by the event can never pass from my mind."

A Ghost's Prediction

Another account, also from the files of the Society for Psychical Research, is unique in that it involves the apparition of one who had passed on a year or more before but who returned to impart news of two impending deaths.

"On Monday, July 31st, 1854," wrote their informant, "I was at Worksop, staying in the house of

Mr. Heming, the then agent there to the Duke of Newcastle. Just as I woke that morning ... I heard the voice of an old schoolfellow, who had been dead at least a year or two, saying, 'Your brother Mark and Harriet are both gone.' These words were echoing in my ears as I woke. I seemed to hear them. My brother then was in America; and both were well when I had last heard of them; but the words respecting him and his wife were so vividly impressed upon my mind that before I left my bedroom I wrote them down, then and there, on a scrap of an old newspaper, having no other paper in the bedroom.

"The voice I seemed to hear, and which at first I thought must have been a kind of dream, had such an effect on me that, though the bell rang for breakfast, I did not go down for some time. And all that day, and for days after, I could not shake it off. I had the strongest impression, and indeed conviction, that my brother was gone.

"That same day I returned to Hull, mentioned the circumstance to my wife, and entered the incident, which had made a deep impression on me, in my diary, which I still have.

"On the 18th of August (it was before the Atlantic telegraph), I received a line from my brother's wife, Harriet, dated August 1st, saying that Mark had just breathed his last, of cholera; after preaching on Sunday, he had been taken ill with cholera on

Monday, and had died on Tuesday morning; that she herself was ill, and that in the event of her death she wished their children should be brought to England. She died the second day after her husband, August 3rd. I immediately started for America, and brought the children home.

"I ought perhaps to add that we had no knowledge of the cholera being in the neighborhood of my brother's parish. My impression was that both he and his wife must, if the voice were true, have been taken away by some railway or steamboat accident. But you should notice that at the moment when I seemed to hear this voice my brother was not dead. He died early next morning, August 1st, and his wife nearly two days later, namely, August 3rd. I do not profess to explain it — I simply state the facts or the phenomena. But the impression made on me was profound and the coincidence itself is remarkable."

A Farewell Kiss

Sometimes the apparition announces itself not only by being seen but with a physical act which can be felt.

"I have a very vivid recollection," a female correspondent to the Society for Psychical Research recounted, "that, towards dawn on the morning of August 3rd, 1867, I was roused from my sleep to find my brother, an officer in the 16th Lancers, then quartered in Madras, standing by the bed. My impression is that he bent over me, kissed me, and passed quietly from the room, making signs to me not to speak, and that I was full of joy, thinking he had returned home unexpectedly, and lay awake till the maid called me, when my first words to her were that my brother had come home and I had seen him. I remember my bitter disappointment when at last made to believe that this was not so, and that it was quite impossible I could have seen him; also that I was scolded and silenced for holding to my story.

"I cannot remember how much time elapsed before the news came by telegram that my brother died suddenly of jungle fever on August 2nd; full particulars did not reach us for weeks later, and it was not till long afterwards that I put two and two together, as the saying is, and, found that, as I then and now firmly believe, my favorite brother came to me at the hour of his death.

A Ghost's Request

An even more striking account was given to me by a, now deceased, friend of mine, Tom McDonough.

It was in the year 1918, in the little town of Lombard, Illinois, that Tom had been attending a party with some other young people at the Garside home, playing the phonograph and dancing.

At the end of the evening Tom left for home and he was about half a block from the Garside house when he noticed that someone was walking beside him. To his surprise, he found that it was Mr. Garside (who had not been at the house during the party) walking in a direction away from his house rather than towards it.

Tom was bewildered when Mr. Garside spoke to him, asking Tom to go back to his house and to tell his family that he was alright.

Utterly confused, Tom asked Mr. Garside why he didn't go back to the house and tell them himself.

"I can't do that, Tom," Mr. Garside responded. "I was on my boat on the north fork of the Chicago River. A fire at the amusement park swept over to my boat and I couldn't get away. Please go back and tell them not to feel bad. Tell them I'm alright."

Tom had never experienced anything like this before and he did not know what to do. "What would his family think," Tom worried, "if Mr. Garside was to return home safe and sound and it turned out that none of this was true?" How in the world could he possibly explain his reason for coming to them with such a story?

When Tom failed to turn back and comply with his request, Mr. Garside vanished.

Tom proceeded on his way home feeling extremely guilty for not having delivered Mr. Garside's message. When he got home Tom telephoned Jean, a young lady with whom he had been keeping company, and who, also, had been at the party that evening.

Although he realized that he was taking a terrible chance of being misunderstood, Tom told Jean exactly what had happened. For the sake of his sanity, he just had to tell somebody, come what may. Jean responded that she thought Tom was wise not to go back to the Garside house, as they would probably not understand and Tom let it go at that.

The next day the news was all over town. Mr. Garside had, indeed, died in the fire at the amusement park. He had been unable to escape the flames when the sail and mast of his boat had collapsed on top of him.

Jean was later to become Tom's wife and, although they had been long since divorced when, years later, I contacted her, Jean confirmed every detail of Tom's account.

Ghosts with a Purpose

Some ghosts appear to remain among us out of a sense of responsibility in the hope of tending to some kind of unfinished business and, once they have achieved their goal, they are never seen again.

The Faithful Chorister

It was almost ten o'clock on a Friday morning in August of 1890 when Edwin Russell felt a blinding bolt of pain flood across his brow. Everything went dark as he collapsed onto the pavement near the corner of Sutter and Mason Streets in San Francisco and, within an hour, the fifty-year-old real estate agent was dead from a cerebral hemorrhage.

A transplanted Englishman who had lived in San Francisco for ten years, Russell had a wonderfully resonate bass singing voice and was greatly appreciated at St. Luke's Episcopal Church where he had long been a faithful and dependable member of the choir. When the wife of St. Luke's rector heard about Russell's death, she sent her brother, a Mr.

Sprague, to the home of Harry E. Reeves, St. Luke's choirmaster, to inform him of Russell's death and to ask him to begin choosing music for his funeral.

When Sprague arrived that afternoon at Reeves' California Street residence, he was met by the choirmaster's sister and niece. They welcomed him into the house, explaining that Reeves was upstairs. The choirmaster had been going over two Te Deums, trying to decide which piece of music to use the following Sunday, when he heard the doorbell ring. Knowing his sister would call him if he was needed, he had decided to lie down and rest for a moment in his bedroom.

But, upon closing his eyes, he was seized by an irresistible impulse to rise and go to the bedroom door. When he opened the door, he saw Russell standing there before him, holding one hand to his forehead and gesturing with a rolled up sheet of music in the other hand. The image was so clear and lifelike that the choirmaster reached out his hand to greet him and was about to speak when the figure turned away, slowly dissolving into the air. Reeves attempted to call out to his friend but he became momentarily paralyzed and fell back against the wall. "My God!" he finally exclaimed.

Upon hearing his words, Sprague and the others rushed upstairs where they found him sitting on the staircase, frightened and confused. "I've just seen Russell," he started to explain.

"But that's impossible," his niece interrupted. "Mr. Sprague just told us that Mr. Russell died this morning."

The blood drained from the choirmaster's face. Slowly he rose to his feet and, without saying another word, went back upstairs to his room. Only then did he relate to them the details of what he had seen.

Perhaps it had merely been a case of telepathy or clairvoyance. Perhaps Reeves had psychically become aware of Russell's death and his mind had, somehow, manufactured a hallucination which might have brought that knowledge into consciousness. But then, perhaps, it was something more. Perhaps the faithful chorister had felt so strongly about his obligation to the choir that, even after death, he had returned to let the choirmaster know that he would be unable to sing on Sunday.

Michael Conley's Ghost

Of course, there are other commitments and responsibilities far more important than one's obligations to a religious or social organization. Consider, for instance, the desire to provide for one's family as best as one can, a desire which, in a case thoroughly investigated and authenticated by the

Society for Psychical Research, suggests a sense of obligation which may continue past death.

In relating the details of the case, I can do no better than to quote from the news story in *The Herald* of Dubuque, Iowa dated February 11th, 1891 which read:

"It will be remembered that on February 2nd, Michael Conley, a farmer living near Ionia, Chickasaw County, was found dead in an outhouse at the Jefferson House. He was carried to Coroner Hoffmann's morgue, where, after an inquest, his body was prepared for shipment to his late home. The old clothes which he wore were covered with filth from the place where he was found, and they were thrown outside the morgue on the ground.

"His son came from Ionia, and took the corpse home. When he reached there, and one of the daughters was told that her father was dead, she fell into a swoon, in which she remained for several hours. When at last she was brought from the swoon, she said, 'Where are Father's old clothes? He has just appeared to me dressed in a white shirt, black clothes, and felt slippers, and told me that after leaving home he sewed a large roll of bills inside his grey shirt with a piece of my red dress, and the money is still there.' In short time she fell into another swoon, and when out of it demanded that

49

someone go to Dubuque and get the clothes. She was deathly sick, and is so yet.

"The entire family considered it only a hallucination, but the physician advised them to get the clothes, as it might set her mind at rest. The son telephoned Coroner Hoffmann, asking if the clothes were still in his possession. He looked and found them in the backyard, although he had supposed they were thrown in the vault, as he had intended. He answered that he still had them, and on being told that the son would come to get them, they were wrapped in a bundle.

"The young man arrived last Monday afternoon, and told Coroner Hoffmann what his sister had said. Mr. Hoffmann admitted that the lady had described the identical burial garb in which her father was clad, even to the slippers, although she never saw him after death, and none of the family had seen more than his face through the coffin lid. Curiosity being fully aroused, they took the grey shirt from the bundle, and within the bosom, found a large roll of bills sewed with a piece of red cloth. The young man said his sister had a red dress exactly like it. The stitches were large and irregular, and looked to be those of a man. The son wrapped up the garments and took them home with him yesterday morning, filled with wonder at the supernatural revelation made to his sister, who is presently lingering between life and death."

The Hidden Grave

In other cases a ghost may remain in order to expose a crime. There exists within the church records of the Scottish town of Fettercairn, in Aberdeenshire, an account of how the Reverend Dr. Rule, who was, at that time, the Chancellor of the University of Edinburgh, stopped for the night in Fettercairn while en route to Aberdeen and solved a mystery.

As the local inn was full at the time, the innkeeper offered Dr. Rule and his servants shelter in an empty house not far from the inn. "I can light you a nice fire, provide candles and blankets and anything else you may require" offered the innkeeper, "but I must warn you that the house is haunted."

That was enough to send the Chancellor's servants off in search of whatever safer accommodations they might find amongst the locals. Dr. Rule, however, was made of sterner stuff and had no qualms about spending the night alone in the house.

That night he undressed, crawled into bed, blew out the candle and promptly fell asleep. All was fine until, a short time later, he awakened and observed the figure of a man approaching the bed. The phantom reached out his hand toward Dr. Rule and removed the candle from a bedside table. The wraith then made his way to the fireplace where it stooped down to light the candle in the still glowing embers of the fire. The specter then turned toward the door, beckoning Dr. Rule to follow.

Now, spending a night in a haunted house was one thing but following a ghost out into that night was something else entirely and Dr. Rule refused to budge from his bed.

The ghost, however, was not to be ignored and, taking up a poker, it thrust the poker into the fire until it glowed red hot. It then laid the poker down on the floor, pointing it directly at the Reverend Doctor.

At this point Dr. Rule realized he had no choice but to do whatever the ghost required and, reluctantly, he followed it out of the bedroom and down a staircase. When they reached the foot of the stairs, the ghost set the candle down onto the floor and the spirit melted away into nothingness.

A lesser man might have fled in terror but Dr. Rule was fascinated and determined to puzzle out the meaning of all that had transpired. Murder, he reasoned must be at the root of it. And, once he had come to that conclusion, he calmly drifted back to sleep.

The next day, he asked the innkeeper if he was aware of any unsolved murders in the vicinity. "No," his host replied.

Still, Dr. Rule was convinced that he was on the right track. He decided to tarry a while in Fettercairn and he arranged that he should preach at the town church that coming Sunday.

His celebrity insured a large turnout and he delivered a sermon on the subject of conscience; a sermon so eloquent and so compelling that, following the service, an old man came up to him, tears flowing from his eyes.

"When I was a young man," the distraught man confessed, "I helped build a house here in town." (That being the very house in which Dr. Rule had encountered the ghost.)

"I got into a quarrel with a fellow worker and we fought. It was an accident. I swear it was only an accident but the other man was killed. I was scared. I didn't know what to do. So, God help me, I dug a hole at the foot of the stairs and I buried him there."

Dr. Rule saw to it that the area at the foot of the staircase was dug up and a skeleton was unearthed. The bones were given a proper church burial and the ghost was never seen again.

The Lost Cantos

Some ghosts seem compelled to appear only once or twice to prevent the loss of an item of importance or to correct an injustice.

Jacopo Alighieri, the son of the poet, Dante Alighieri, wrote that, when his father died, thirteen cantos of his *Divine Comedy* were missing from his manuscripts and, despite an exhaustive search, no one had he slightest idea as to where they might be. Then one night he dreamed that his father appeared to him and told him of the location of a drawer in which he would find the lost manuscripts. The next morning, Jacopo found a drawer in exactly the place his father had said it would be and inside were the missing manuscripts of all thirteen cantos.

To Rectify an Injustice

A more recent case was reported by William Oliver Stevens in his book, *Unbidden Guests*, in which he recounts an incident related to him by a former United States government official who, while naturally sensitive to psychic influences, had become especially interested in paranormal phenomena while a student of the psychologist and philosopher, William James, at Harvard.

This official, whom Stevens calls "H." in order to preserve his anonymity, was working at his typewriter one Sunday when the apparition of a man, a man he had never seen before, appeared before him in his Boston apartment.

The apparition spoke, identifying himself as the father of a man whom H. had met only four times. The ghost said he had come to H. to ask that he transmit a message to his son, a message necessary to rectify an injustice he had visited upon his second wife.

When the father had announced that he intended to marry his stenographer, both his son and his daughter had vociferously argued against the marriage, accusing the woman of only being after their father's money. As his children's animosity continued after the wedding, his new wife attempted to end their hostility by signing an agreement to not accept more than ten thousand dollars from her husband's estate, should he predecease her.

As the estate turned out to be much larger than had been supposed and the ghost felt that ten thousand dollars would not be enough to meet his widow's needs, he desired that H. convince his children to provide a more appropriate settlement for their stepmother.

When H. passed the ghost's message on to the son, the request was met with laughter. Nothing further, the son declared, would be given to the widow.

The ghost, however, angry with his son, was not to be denied and appeared again to H. in his apartment the following Sunday morning and identified a bank in Chicago, saying, "Tell him this time that in the bank in Chicago I have a safe deposit box with a sum of money in it of which he knows nothing. Tell him to go and get it."

H. reluctantly imparted the new message to the son and, again, the son responded with derision.

Now the ghost became extremely angry and appeared to H. saying, "I'll make him go to Chicago! There is something my children don't know and will not be able to ignore. Tell my son they are the offspring of my second marriage. Before I married their mother I had been secretly married to a woman I divorced for infidelity. The papers for that are in my strongbox."

He gave H. the number of his Chicago safe deposit box as well as informing him that his son would find inside ten thousand dollars in government bonds for which he gave H. the serial numbers.

When H. delivered this message, the son, again, treated it with distain but thought he had best ask his father's brother and business associate if he knew of the secret marriage.

Although the brother denied any knowledge of such a marriage, the son was now intrigued enough to contact the Chicago bank and he was stunned to learn that his father did, indeed, have a safe deposit box there.

Upon traveling to Chicago and opening the strongbox, he found, not only the ten thousand dollars in government bonds with the serial numbers given to him by the ghost, but papers documenting the secret marriage.

Still, the son and his sister had doubts and required one last test. H. was asked to examine a number of family photographs and, from them, to identify their father.

H. was baffled. No one in any the photographs matched exactly the face of the apparition who had sent him out on this strange journey. In frustration, H. pointed to the photograph of a man with a beard and said, "If it weren't for that beard, I would say that was the man I saw."

"Now I believe!" exclaimed the son. "Father always wore a beard but he shaved it off a week or two before he died."

The ghost's son and daughter agreed to provide a more substantial financial settlement for their stepmother and their father's ghost was never seen again.

"Ye'll Sune Ken!"

A final, highly dramatic case comes from the *Proceedings of the Society for Psychical Research*, an account sent to them by a gentleman of impeccable credentials, all of the details of which were backed up by an accompanying statement from the man's wife.

"I am the owner of a very old mechanical business in Glasgow," the gentleman reported, "with for twenty years past a branch in London, where I have resided for that period, and in both of which places my professional reputation is of the highest order.

"Some thirty-five years ago I took into my employment a tender, delicate looking boy, Robert Mackenzie, who, after some three or four years' service, suddenly left, as I found out afterwards, through the selfish advice of older hands, who practiced this frightening away systematically to keep wages from being lowered, a common device, I believe, among workmen in limited trades.

"Passing the gate of the great workhouse in the Parliamentary Road, a few years afterwards, my eye was caught by a youth of some eighteen years of age ravenously devouring a piece of dry bread on the public street, and bearing all the appearance of being in a chronic state of starvation. Fancying I knew his features, I asked if his name were not Mackenzie. He at once became much excited, addressed me by name, and informed me that he had no employment; that his father and mother, who formerly supported him, were now both inmates of the "poorhouse," to which he himself had no claim for admission, being young and without any bodily disqualification for work, and that he was literally homeless and starving. The matron, he informed me, gave him daily a piece of dry bread, but durst not, under the rules, give him regular maintenance.

"In an agony of grief he deplored his ever leaving me under evil advice, and on my unexpectedly offering to take him back he burst into a transport of thanks, such as I cannot describe. Suffice it to say that he resumed his work, and that, under the circumstances, I did everything in my power to facilitate his progress. All this was mere matter of course; but the distinction between it and the common relations of master and servant was this, that on every occasion of my entering the workshop he never, so far as possible, took off his eyes from following my movements. Let me look towards him at any moment, there was the pale, sympathetic face with the large and wistful eyes, literally yearning towards me, as Smike's did towards Nicholas Nickleby.

"I seemed to be 'the polar star of his existence,' and this intensity of gratitude never appeared to lessen in degree through lapse of time. Beyond this he never ventured to express his feelings. His manhood, as it were, his individuality and self-assertion, seemed to have been crushed out of him by privations. I was apparently his sole thought and consideration, saving the more common concerns of daily life.

"In 1862 I settled in London, and have never been in Glasgow since. Robert Mackenzie, and my workmen generally, gradually lost their individuality in my recollection.

"About ten to twelve years ago my employees had their annual soiree and ball. This was always held, year after year, on a Friday evening. Mackenzie, ever shy and distant as usual, refused to mingle in the festivities, and begged of my foreman to be permitted to serve at the buffet. All went off well, and the Saturday was held as a succeeding day of festival. All this, however, I only learned after what I am now about to relate.

"On the Tuesday morning following, immediately before 8 a.m., in my house on Campden Hill, I had the following manifestation I cannot call it a dream; but let me use the common phraseology. I dreamt, but with no vagueness as in common dreams, no blurring of outline or rapid passages from one thing disconnectedly to another, that I was seated at a desk, engaged in a business conversation with an unknown gentleman, who stood on my right hand. Towards me, in front, advanced Robert Mackenzie, and feeling annoyed, I addressed him with some asperity, asking him if he did not see that I was engaged. He retired a short distance with exceeding reluctance, turned again to approach me, as if most desirous for an immediate colloquy, when I spoke to him still more sharply as to his want of manners. On this, the person with whom I was conversing took his leave, and Mackenzie once more came forward.

"On looking at Mackenzie I was struck by the peculiar appearance of his countenance. It was of an indescribable bluish-pale color, and on his forehead appeared spots which seemed like blots of sweat. For this I could not account.

"'What is all this, Robert?' I asked somewhat angrily. 'Did you not see I was engaged?'

"'Yes, sir,' he replied; 'but I must speak with you at once.'

"'What about?' I said. 'What is it that can be so important?'

"'I wish to tell you, sir,' he answered, 'that I am accused of doing a thing I did not do, and that I want you to know it, and to tell you so, and that you are to forgive me for what I am blamed for, because I am innocent. I did not do the thing they say I did.'

"I said, 'What?' getting same answer. I then naturally asked, 'But how can I forgive you if you do not tell me what you are accused of?'

"I can never forget the emphatic manner of his answer in the Scottish dialect,' Ye'll sune ken' (You'll soon know.) This question and the answer were repeated at least twice. I am certain the answer was repeated thrice, in the most fervid tone. On that I awoke, and was in that state of surprise and bewilderment which such a remarkable dream ... might induce, and was wondering what it all meant, when my wife burst into my bedroom, much excited, and holding an open letter in her hand, exclaimed, 'Oh, James, here's a terrible end to the workmen's ball. Robert Mackenzie has committed suicide!'

"With now a full conviction of the meaning of the vision, I at once quietly and firmly said, 'No, he has not committed suicide.'

"'How can you possibly know that?'

"'Because he has just been here to tell me.'

"By the following post my manager informed me that he was wrong in writing me of suicide. That on Saturday night, Mackenzie, on going home, had lifted a small black bottle containing *aqua fortis* (used for staining the wood of birdcages,) believing this to be whisky, and pouring out a wine-glassful, had drunk it off at a gulp, dying on the Sunday in great agony. Here then, was the solution of his being innocent of what he was accused of, suicide, seeing that he had inadvertently drunk *aqua fortis*, a deadly poison.

"Still pondering upon the peculiar color of his countenance, it struck me to consult some authorities on the symptoms of poisoning by *aqua fortis*, and in Mr. J. H. Walsh's *Domestic Medicine and Surgery*, page, 172, I found these words under symptoms of poisoning by sulphuric acid. ... 'The skin covered with a cold sweat; countenance livid and expressive of dreadful suffering. *Aqua fortis* produces the same effect as sulphuric, the only difference being that the external stains, if any, are yellow instead of brown.' This refers to indication of sulphuric acid, 'generally outside of the mouth, in the shape of brown spots.'

"Having no desire to accommodate my facts to this scientific description, I give the quotations freely, only at the same time stating that previously to reading the passage in Mr. Walsh's book, I had not the slightest knowledge of these symptoms, and I consider that they agree fairly and sufficiently with what I saw, a livid face covered with a remarkable sweat, and having spots (particularly on the forehead), which, in my dream, I thought great blots of perspiration. It seems not a little striking that I had no previous knowledge of these symptoms, and yet should take note of them.

"I have little remark to make beyond this, that in speaking of this matter, to me very affecting and solemn, I have been quite disgusted by skeptics treating it as a hallucination, in so far as that my dream must have been on the Wednesday morning, being that after the receipt of my manager's letter informing me of the supposed suicide. This explanation is too absurd to require a serious answer. My manager first heard of the death on the Monday, wrote me on that day as above and on the Tuesday wrote again explaining the true facts. The dream was on the Tuesday morning, immediately before the 8 a.m. post delivery, hence the thrice emphatic 'Ye'll sune ken.' I attribute the whole to Mackenzie's yearning gratitude for being rescued from a deplorable state of starvation, and his earnest desire to stand well in my opinion, I have colored nothing, and leave my readers to draw their own conclusions."

Crisis Ghosts

Sometimes, in the midst of a crisis, an image of that event can be psychically transmitted through time and space to a loved one or even to an unrelated percipient creating what is called a "crisis ghost."

The Death of Edmund Dunn

On October 24th, 1889, Edmund Dunn was working as a fireman on the *Wolf*, a steam-powered tugboat serving ships in the Harbor of Chicago, when at around three o'clock in the morning, while adjusting a towline, he either fell or was caught by the towline and hurled overboard and drowned. About three weeks later his body, having floated to the surface, was discovered near the place where the accident had occurred.

In a statement sent to the Society for Physical Research, his sister, Mrs. Agnes Paquet, wrote the following:

"I arose about the usual hour on the morning of the accident, probably about six o'clock. I had slept well throughout the night, had no dreams or sudden awakenings. I awoke feeling gloomy and depressed, which feeling I could not shake off. After breakfast my husband went to his work, and, at the proper time, the children were gotten ready and sent to school, leaving me alone in the house. Soon after this I decided to steep and drink some tea, hoping it would relieve me of the gloomy feelings aforementioned. I went into the pantry, took down the tea canister, and as I turned around my brother Edmund — or his exact image — stood before me and only a few feet away. The apparition stood with back toward me, or, rather, partially so, and was in the act of falling forward — away from me — seemingly impelled by two ropes or a loop of rope drawing against his legs. The vision lasted but a moment, disappearing over a low railing or bulwark, but was very distinct. I dropped the tea, clasped my hands to my face, and exclaimed, 'My God! Ed is drowned.'

"At about half-past 10 a.m. my husband received a telegram from Chicago, announcing the drowning of my brother. When he arrived home he said to me, 'Ed is sick in hospital at Chicago; I have just received a telegram,' to which I replied, 'Ed is drowned; I saw him go overboard.' I then gave him a minute description of what I had seen. I stated that my brother, as I saw him, was bareheaded, had on a heavy, blue sailor's shirt, no coat, and that he went over the rail or bulwark. I noticed that his pants' legs were rolled up enough to show the white lining inside. I also described the appearance of the boat at the point where my brother went overboard.

"I am not nervous, and neither before nor since have I had any experience in the least degree similar to that above related.

"My brother was not subject to fainting or vertigo."

Mrs. Paquet's statement was verified by one from her husband which read as follows:

"At about 10:30 o'clock a.m., October 24th, 1889, I received a telegram from Chicago, announcing the drowning of my brother-in-law, Edmund Dunn, at three o'clock that morning. I went directly home, and, wishing to break the force of the sad news I had to convey to my wife, I said to her: 'Ed is sick in hospital at Chicago; I have just received a telegram.' To which she replied: 'Ed is drowned; I saw him go overboard.' She then described to me the appearance and dress of her brother as described in her statement; also the appearance of the boat.

"I started at once for Chicago, and when I arrived there I found the appearance of that part of the vessel described by my wife to be exactly as she had described it, though she had never seen the vessel; and the crew verified my wife's description of her brother's dress, except that they thought that he had his hat on at the time of the accident. They said that

Mr. Dunn had purchased a pair of pants a few days before the accident occurred, and as they were a trifle long, he had worn them rolled up, showing the white lining as seen by my wife.

"The captain of the tug, who was at the wheel at the time of the accident, seemed reticent. He thought my brother-in-law was taken with a fainting fit or vertigo and fell over backward; but a sailor (Frank Yemont) told a friend of mine that he (Yemont) stood on the bow of the vessel that was being towed and saw the accident. He stated that my brother-in-law was caught by the tow-line and thrown overboard, as described by my wife. I think that the captain, in his statement, wished to avoid responsibility, as he had no right to order a fireman — my brother-in-law's occupation — to handle the tow-line.

"My brother-in-law was never, to my knowledge, subject to fainting or vertigo."

A Stumble on the Steps

A far less traumatic case was sent to the Society for Psychical Research involving a lady who wished to be referred to only as "Mrs. B." and her friend, Mrs. E. A. Conner, a lady well known at the time as a writer and speaker.

On January 15th, 1889, Mrs. Conner received the following letter which had been sent on the previous day:

"My Dear Friend,

"I know you will be surprised to receive a note from me so soon, but not more so than I was today when you were shown to me clairvoyantly, in a somewhat embarrassed position. I doubt very much if there was any truth in it, nevertheless, will relate it, and leave you to laugh at the idea of it.

"I was sitting in my room sewing, this afternoon, about two o'clock, when what should I see but your own dear self; but, Heavens! in what a position. Now, I don't want to excite your curiosity too much, or try your patience too long, so will come to the point at once. You were falling up the front steps in the yard. You had on your black skirt and velvet waist, your little straw bonnet, and in your hand were some papers. When you fell, your hat went in one direction and the papers in another. You got up very quickly, put on your bonnet, picked up the papers, and lost no time getting into the house. You did not appear to be hurt, but looked somewhat mortified. It was all so plain to me that I had ten notions to one to dress myself and come over and see if it were true, but finally concluded that a sober, industrious woman like yourself would not be stumbling around at that rate, and thought I'd best not go on a wild goose chase. Now, what do you think of such a vision as that? Is there any possible truth in it? I feel almost ready to scream with laughter whenever I think, of it; you did look too funny, spreading yourself out in the front yard. 'Great was the fall thereof.'

"I can distinctly call to mind the house in which you live, but for the life of me I cannot tell whether there are any steps from the sidewalk into the yard, as I saw them, or not.

"Now do tell me, dear, if I saw correctly or not, or if the thing was shown me simply to give me something to laugh about?

"Hope you got home last night without any adventures. And now 'Good-night."

Upon receiving the letter, Mrs. Connor revealed to a friend who happened to call on her that day that the accident had, indeed, occurred exactly, "in every essential particular," as had been related in the letter.

Mrs. Connor wrote, in response to questions put to her by Frederic W. H. Myers of the Society for Psychical Research:

"I was writing that day in the Congressional Library. I finished my work, and passed out through the Capitol Building. As I did so, I glanced at the large clock in the hall, and it lacked 20 minutes to three. It was not more than a minute till I reached the steps where I fell, so that it must have been within a few seconds of 19 minutes to three. I have no means of ascertaining whether the vision preceded the accident.

"To me the most convincing proof of the correctness of the vision is a sentence you will find like this, if I remember right, in the letter: 'I do not know if there are steps from the sidewalk to the yard.' The queer fact is that there were two steps from the sidewalk to the yard, the street having been cut down. On the top one of these two steps, in the yard, I stumbled. Mrs. B. had never seen this house, I having only removed thither a few days before."

Dr. Young's Dream

While the foregoing cases occurred to women who were wide awake at the time of their visions, crisis visions often come in the form of a dream.

On a Monday night in December, 1836, Dr. A. K. Young, of The Terrace, County Monaghan, Ireland dreamed that he was standing at the gate of an estate many miles from his home. With him were a woman with a basket hanging from her arm, four men whom he recognized as his tenants and other men who were strangers, some of whom were brutally attacking one of his tenants, a man identified in the account only as H. W. In the dream, Dr. Young sprang to his tenant's defense.

"I struck violently at the man on my left," Dr. Young was to later write, "and then with greater violence at the man's face to my right. Finding to my surprise that I did not knock him down, I struck again and again, with all the violence of a man frenzied at the sight of my poor friend's murder. To my great amazement I saw that my arms, although visible to my eye, were without substance; and the bodies of the men I struck at and my own came close together after each blow through the shadowy arms I struck with. My blows were delivered with more extreme violence than I think I ever exerted; but I became painfully convinced of my incompetency. I have no consciousness of what happened, after this feeling of insubstantiality came upon me."

The following morning Dr. Young awoke to muscles which were stiff and sore and his wife told him that she had been frightened by his thrashing about during the night, lunging about with his arms "as if fighting for his life." He told her the details of his dream and Wednesday morning he received a letter from his estate agent informing him that his tenant, H. W. had been found at the location Dr. Young had seen in his dream unable to speak and suffering from a fractured skull.

Dr. Young set out for town and requested the senior magistrate to order the questioning of the three men he had recognized in the dream. All three men gave accounts identical to each others' testimony which also matched the events in Dr. Young's dream. All three men also identified the woman with the basket who, upon questioning, offered a similar account.

The four witnesses all agreed that, between eleven o'clock and midnight, they had been walking together to their homes "when they were overtaken by three strangers, two of whom savagely assaulted H. W., while the other prevented his friends from interfering."

While H. W. recovered from his injuries, it was said that he "was never the same afterwards" and eventually he left Ireland.

Dr. Young would later write, "I pass the spot where I was conscious of the attack very frequently; and I can point with my finger to within a foot or two of where I fought, and the positions of all the parties present. Had not my wife been present and awake when I was so profoundly asleep, and witnessed the amazing and alarming violence of the blows I made, (a matter she spoke of afterwards to me more than once, with terror,) I never could have accounted for the very wretched feeling of weariness, prostration, and pain with which I got from my bed on the next morning."

Ghosts of the Living

Numerous, carefully documented cases suggest that it is possible for the spirit of a living person to temporarily leave the physical body and travel to another location miles away where it can be seen and physically interact with another person creating a "ghost of the living."

The Fiancée's Ghost

The Reverend P. H. Newnham described himself as "an utter skeptic, in the true sense of the word." Still, he felt compelled to record a strange experience which was reported in Edmund Gurney, Frederic W. H. Myers and Frank Podmore's groundbreaking 1886 work, *Phantoms of the Living*.

"In March, 1854," Reverend Newnham wrote, "I was up at Oxford, keeping my last term, in lodgings. I was subject to violent neuralgic headaches, which always culminated in sleep. One evening, about 8 p.m., I had an unusually violent one. When it became unendurable, about 9 p.m., I went into my bedroom, and flung myself, without undressing, on the bed, and soon fell asleep.

"I then had a singularly clear and vivid dream, all the incidents of which are still as clear to my memory as ever. I dreamed that I was stopping with the family of the lady who subsequently became my wife. All the younger ones had gone to bed, and I stopped chatting to the father and mother, standing up by the fireplace. Presently I bade them goodnight, took my candle, and went off to bed. On arriving in the hall, I perceived that my fiancée had been detained downstairs, and was only then near the top of the staircase. I rushed upstairs, overtook her on the top step, and passed my two arms round her waist, under her arms, from behind. Although I was carrying my candle in my left hand, when I ran upstairs, this did not, in my dream, interfere with this gesture.

"On this I woke, and a clock in the house struck ten almost immediately afterwards.

"So strong was the impression of the dream that I wrote a detailed account of it next morning to my fiancée.

"Crossing my letter, not in answer to it, I received a letter from the lady in question."

"Were you thinking about me," his fiancée had written, "very specially, last night, just about ten o'clock? For, as I was going upstairs to bed, I distinctly heard your footsteps on the stairs, and felt you put your arms round my waist."

Mrs. Newnham corroborated her husband's memory of the event, writing, "I remember distinctly the circumstance which my husband has described as corresponding with his dream. I was on my way up to bed, as usual, about ten o'clock, and on reaching the first landing I heard distinctly the footsteps of the gentleman to whom I was engaged, quickly mounting the stairs after me, and then I as plainly felt him put his arms round my waist. So strong an impression did this make upon me that I wrote the very next morning to the gentleman, asking if he had been particularly thinking of me at ten o'clock the night before, and to my astonishment I received (at the same time that my letter would reach him) a letter from him describing his dream, in almost the same words that I had used in describing my impression of his presence."

A Visit at Sea

In the year 1891, an even more impressive account by a Mr. S. R. Wilmot of what was then referred to as a "psychical excursion" was published in the *Proceedings of the Society for Psychical Research.*

"On October 3rd, 1863," Mr. Wilmot wrote, "I sailed from Liverpool for New York, on the steamer,

City of Limerick, of the Inman line, Captain Jones commanding. On the evening of the second day out, soon after leaving Kinsale Head, a severe storm began, which lasted for nine days. During this time we saw neither sun nor stars nor any vessel; the bulwarks on the weather bow were carried away, one of the anchors broke loose from its lashings, and did considerable damage before it could be secured, and several stout storm sails, though closely reefed, were carried away, and the booms broken.

"Upon the night following the eighth day of the storm the tempest moderated a little, and for the first time since leaving port I enjoyed refreshing sleep. Toward morning I dreamed that I saw my wife, whom I had left in the United States, come to the door of my state-room, clad in her night dress. At the door she seemed to discover that I was not the only occupant of the room, hesitated a little, then advanced to my side, stooped down and kissed me, and after gently caressing me for a few moments, quietly withdrew.

"Upon waking I was surprised to see my fellow passenger, whose berth was above mine, but not directly over it — owing to the fact that our room was at the stern of the vessel — leaning upon his elbow, and looking fixedly at me. 'You're a pretty fellow,' said he at length, 'to have a lady come and visit you in this way.' I pressed him for an explanation, which he at first declined to give, but at length related what he had seen while wide awake, lying in his berth. It exactly corresponded with my dream.

"This gentleman's name was William J. Tait, and he had been my room-mate in the passage out, in the preceding July, on the Cunard steamer, *Olympus*; a native of England, and son of a clergyman of the Established Church. He had for a number of years lived in Cleveland, in the State of Ohio, where he held the position of librarian of the Associated Library. He was at this time perhaps fifty years of age — by no means in the habit of practical joking, but a sedate and very religious man, whose testimony upon any subject could be taken unhesitatingly.

"The incident seemed so strange to me that I questioned him about it, and upon three separate occasions, the last one shortly before reaching port, Mr. Tait repeated to me the same account of what he had witnessed.

"The day after landing I went by rail to Watertown, Connecticut, where my children and my wife had been for some time, visiting her parents. Almost her first question, when we were alone together, was, 'Did you receive a visit from me a week ago Tuesday?'

"'A visit from you?' said I, 'we were more than a thousand miles at sea.'

"'I know it,' she replied, 'but it seemed to me that I visited you.'

"'It would be impossible,' said I. 'Tell me what makes you think so.'

"My wife then told me that on account of the severity of the weather and the reported loss of the *Africa*, which sailed for Boston on the same day that we left Liverpool for New York, and had gone ashore at Cape Race, she had been extremely anxious about me. On the night previous, the same night when the storm had just begun to abate, she had lain awake for a long time thinking of me, and about four o'clock in the morning it seemed to her that she went out to seek me. Crossing the wide and stormy sea, she came at length to a low, black steamship, whose side she went up, and then descending into the cabin, passed through it to the stern until she came to my stateroom.

"'Tell me,' said she, 'do they ever have state-rooms like the one I saw, where the upper berth extends further back than the under one? A man was in the upper berth, looking right at me, and for a moment I was afraid to go in, but soon I went up to the side of your berth, bent down and kissed you, and embraced you, and then went away.'

"The description given by my wife of the steamship was correct in all particulars, though she had never seen it.

"I only spoke of my dream and Mr. Tait's experience to my sister who was with me then, as I could not quite divest myself of the thought that Mr. Tait might have invented his part from witnessing something unusual in me while asleep.

"I did not mention these things to any but my sister till after reaching home and learning what I did from my wife. That astonished me; it almost took my breath away."

Mr. Wilmot's sister backed up the validity of her brother's account with the following statement sent to the Society for Psychical Research:

"In regard to my brother's strange experience on our homeward voyage in the *Limerick* — I remember Mr. Tait's asking me, one morning (when assisting me to the breakfast table, for the cyclone was raging fearfully), if I had been in last night to see my brother; and my astonishment at the question, as he shared the same state-room.

"At my 'No, why?' he said he saw some woman, in white, who went up to my brother (who was too seasick to leave his berth for several days.)

"I soon went in to see my brother, who told me that Mr. Tait had wondered at my coming in to see him, and I think he said he had dreamed of seeing his wife there, but in the imminent danger that loomed over us, I did not fix my mind on their after conversations."

The Hypnotist's Experiment

A frighteningly successful experiment concerning a "psychical excursion" was carried out in 1855 by an amateur hypnotist named John Moule, who wished to see if he could project his spirit to one of his most sensitive hypnotic subjects.

"I chose for this purpose," he wrote, "a young lady, a Miss Drasey, and stated that someday I intended to visit her wherever she might be although the place might be unknown to me; and told her, if anything particular should occur, to note the time, and when she called at my house again, to state if anything had occurred.

"One day about two months after (I not having seen her in the interval) I was by myself in my chemical factory, Redman's Row, Mile End, London, all alone, and I determined to try the experiment, the lady being in Dalston, about three miles off. I stood up, raised my hands, and willed to act upon the lady. I soon felt that I had expended energy. I immediately sat down in a chair, and went to sleep.

"I then saw in a dream my friend coming down the kitchen stairs, where I dreamt I was. She saw me and suddenly exclaimed, 'Oh! Mr. Moule,' and fainted away. This I dreamt, and then awoke.

"I thought very little about it, supposing I had had an ordinary dream; but about three weeks after she came to my house, and related to my wife the singular occurrence of her seeing me sitting in the kitchen, where she then was, and that she fainted away and nearly dropped some dishes she had in her hands.

"All this I saw exactly in my dream so that I described the kitchen furniture, and where I sat, as perfectly as if I had been there, though I had never been in the house. I gave many details, and she said, 'It is just as if you had been there.' After this, she made me promise that I would never do it again as she would never feel happy with the idea of me appearing to her."

The Phantom Cicerone

The foregoing accounts pale, however, in comparison to an account published by Jessie Adelaide Middleton in her *White Ghost Book*.

"The following story," Miss Middleton recalled, "was related to me by Mrs. Charles Mossop, of Peterborough Road, Harrow-on-the-Hill, who has kindly given me permission to use her name and address and vouches for its authenticity.

"The events related in it happened to a friend of hers, an officer of high rank in the Army, and whose name is well known to me and to the public in general. Here is the story:

"A young cadet of nineteen, having completed his course at the Royal Military Academy and been appointed to the Royal Engineers, was spending a few days in London before joining. One night he made up his mind to go to some place of amusement, and putting on his dress-clothes, called a hansom and drove to a music-hall in the West End.

"During the evening an elderly gentleman, of extremely aristocratic appearance, entered into conversation with him and took considerable interest in his account of himself and his hopes and ambitions.

"The boy frankly told the stranger that he wanted 'to see a little life' before he went abroad, and the latter offered to be his cicerone for the night and introduce him to places to which he could not otherwise hope to be admitted.

"Delighted at the prospect, and fascinated by the older man's charm and conversation, the boy gratefully accepted the invitation; and they went off to supper at one of the best restaurants.

"After supper — at which the boy drank only lemon squash — they went to several gambling-dens and night clubs, at some of which it was necessary to give a password, and everywhere the man was received and treated with the utmost deference. They did not actually join in any of the doings at the places they visited, but, both being particularly refined and fastidious, preferred to play the part of lookers on.

"Towards three o'clock in the morning the man asked the boy where he was staying, and hearing that it was in a direction that would not take him out of his way, suggested that they should walk together to St. James's Square, where the speaker lived.

"It was a very fine night in summer, and the cool air, after the hot, vitiated atmosphere of the night clubs, was deliciously fresh. The two walked together in the direction of St. James's Square, and as they passed St. James's Church, Piccadilly, the clocks struck three, and the elder man stopped to wind up his watch.

"They walked down a side street into St. James's Square, and at the door of one of the large houses in the square the stranger took out his latch-key and said good night, adding that he hoped the boy had had a pleasant evening. With profuse thanks for his kindness, the boy asked permission to call with his father next day, saying he was sure his father would like to thank him in person. Permission was given and cards exchanged. The man then entered the house and the boy went home.

"Next day he told his father what had happened, and they arranged to call at the house in St. James's Square that afternoon.

"When they did so the door was opened by a butler, who seemed much distressed. After some conversation the butler told them that his master had died at three-fifteen that morning, that he had been bedridden for four months previously, and unconscious for twelve hours before his death.

"The boy, being unable to believe the story, asked the butler to show him a photograph of his master, which he did, and the boy instantly recognized it.

"The owner of the house had been a man well known in society, and his funeral a few days later was attended by a large number of members of the fashionable world."

Poltergeists

Unexplainable bangs and thumps in the middle of the night. Doors opening and closing of their own accord. Objects thrown through the air. Furniture moving about without rhyme or reason. These may be signs of the mysterious phenomenon known as the poltergeist.

The mischievous and sometimes dangerous poltergeist, a German word meaning "noisy or boisterous ghost," is unusual among the various forms of paranormal phenomena which we tend to ascribe to ghosts in that it is never seen. However, its dramatic manifestations leave no doubt as to its presence.

A Nevada City Poltergeist

A retired deputy sheriff in my hometown of Nevada City, California related to me the details of an incident which he, himself, had witnessed concerning a stately Victorian home dating back to the town's California Gold Rush beginnings, a home which belonged to a family which regularly closed up the house during the winter months and spent those months living in the San Francisco Bay Area.

It was a cold night in January or February, not all that long ago, when the alarm went off in their securely locked and unoccupied house. When the police arrived they observed that the French doors off a second floor bedroom were standing wide open. As the owners of the house had left a set of keys with the police, the officers were able to enter and search the house thoroughly. Once they had assured themselves that no one was in the house, the police closed and secured the French doors, locked up the house and returned to the police station.

Forty-five minutes to an hour later, the alarm went off again and, again, the police made their way back to the house. Again, the French doors were standing wide open and, once again, the police made their way to the bedroom. One of the officers then noticed a man's belt lying on the bed and decided that he would tie the handles of the doors together with the belt. This being done, the police, again, locked up the house and left.

Forty-five minutes to an hour later, the alarm went off for a third time and, for a third time, the police made their way back to the house. For the third time, the French doors were standing wide open. When they entered the bedroom, the belt was back on the bed where they had initially found it.

The Holbrooke Hotel Poltergeists

Only a few miles away, in the California Gold Rush era town of Grass Valley, the previously mentioned Holbrooke Hotel has long been the scene of formidable poltergeist activity. In the Holbrooke's kitchen culinary utensils have been known to swing back and forth on their racks, sometimes even rising high off of their hooks, floating in midair, and the water taps in both the kitchen and the ladies' room have been repeatedly turned on full blast by unseen hands.

The vintage elevator has often been known to move from floor to floor late at night, when all of the hotel's guests are fast asleep; its door opening to reveal no one inside.

A picture and a heavy mirror have reportedly floated free from the nails from which they had been suspended. Heavy pieces of furniture have thrown themselves into a pile blocking a staircase landing. Lights and televisions in guests' rooms have been known to turn themselves on and off by themselves. Curtains have been known to fly out from the wall wrapping themselves around an unsuspecting guest while other guests, careful to have securely locked their door before leaving their room, have been startled upon their return to find the door standing wide open. And, late at night, the door knob in a particular room has been known to turn back and forth and the door, itself, has been known to shake violently.

And then here was the evening the entire hotel appeared to be under assault as a violent pounding was heard on each of the Holbrooke's windows; an ominous rapping which began at the front entrance and, then, raced around the entire building. Although hotel staff rushed out to apprehend whoever might be perpetrating a prank, no flesh and blood prankster was ever discovered.

Some parapsychologists suggest that such events are due not to ghosts but, instead, to unconscious and uncontrollable psychokinetic energy flowing from an adolescent experiencing a period of extreme emotional stress. But such a theory could hardly account for a hotel staffed entirely by adults or a securely locked and unoccupied house. And how could such a theory explain a poltergeist which clearly shows signs of being a ghost with a distinct personality?

Room 9 at the Holbrooke is considered to be one of the hotels most haunted rooms. From time to time, spirits have been seen passing through its locked door. The lights have been known to turn on by themselves in the locked and unoccupied room and guests have sometimes heard the lyrical voice of a woman singing; perhaps the voice of the ghostly maid, a most fastidious housekeeper, who has been known to sometimes pick up after sloppy guests.

A female guest, an army officer, after spending the night in Room 9, asked the hotel manager the next morning, "Do people come into the rooms at night and do things?"

"I certainly hope not!" the manager replied. "Why do you ask?"

"I'm a bit of a slob," the lady explained. Her way of unpacking was simply to dump the entire contents of her luggage out onto the floor and that was what she had done. Upon awakening that morning, however, she found that all of her clothing and other personal items had either been hung up in an armoire, been placed neatly in the dresser drawers or had been carefully arranged upon the top of the dresser.

The army officer's experience would not be at all unique. Guests often tell of seeing the ghostly maid, a short woman wearing a long dress with a bustle, her blonde hair pulled back into a bun, tidying up the room in the middle of the night or making the bed while the guest is still in it.

Though highly efficient and helpful to the guests of whom she approves, the ghostly maid can be roused to anger regarding those of whom she does not approve. It is said that on one occasion a guest who had carefully unpacked her luggage upon her arrival was dismayed, upon awakening in the morning, to find that all of her belongings had been roughly crammed back into her suitcase!

The Enniscorthy Poltergeist

An extremely striking example of poltergeist activity was presented in a paper to the Society for Psychical research by Professor W. Barrett, a Fellow of the Royal Society, regarding a house in Court Street, Enniscorthy, County Wexford, Ireland where, in 1910, a man named Redmond lived with his wife.

The couple supplemented their income by taking in boarders; three young men, John Randall, George Sinnott and another boy identified only as Richard, who slept in a large room containing two beds situated on the second floor above the kitchen.

It was on the night of Thursday, July 7th, that began what turned out to be a three week long ordeal which would result in Randall losing ten and a half pounds in weight. All seemed normal that night until, without warning, Randall, having been snug in bed, felt the bedclothes being pulled away. Thinking that his roommates were indulging in a prank, he shouted for them to stop. When his companions pleaded innocence and a match was struck, the bedclothes were found to be at the window and it was discovered that the other bed (which was so large that it normally took two persons to move it) had moved from its normal position.

The bed was quickly repositioned and the bedclothes retrieved but, once the lights were blown out, as Randall was to later report in a signed statement, "It wasn't long until we heard some hammering in the room tap-tap-tap-like. This lasted for a few minutes, getting quicker and quicker. When it got very quick, their bed started to move out across the room.

"We then struck a match and got the lamp. We searched the room thoroughly, and could find nobody. Nobody had come in the door. We called the man of the house (Mr. Redmond.) He came into the room, saw the bed, and told us to push it back and get into bed (he thought all the time one of us was playing the trick on the other.)

"I said I wouldn't stay in the other bed by myself, so I got in with the others; we put out the light again, and it had only been a couple of minutes out when the bed ran out on the floor with the three of us. Richard struck a match again, and this time we all got up and put on our clothes; we had got a terrible fright and couldn't stick it any longer. We told the man of the house we would sit up in the room till daylight. During the time we were sitting in the room we could hear footsteps leaving the kitchen and coming up the stairs; it would stop on the landing outside the door, and wouldn't come into the room. The footsteps and noises continued through the house until daybreak."

Although the footsteps and tapping sounds continued throughout the following night, nothing else occurred.

On the night of Monday, July 11th the largest bed, now occupied by all three men, again rolled out from its normal position by the window and, by the light of a lamp which they kept burning throughout the night, the terrified men saw a chair "dance" out into the middle of the room.

On Thursday, July 14th, not only were the events of Monday night repeated but one of the men found himself rudely thrown out of the bed.

On each successive night in which they slept in the room, such events continued unabated.

On Friday, July 29th, Randall reported that "the bed turned up on one side and threw us out on the floor, and before we were thrown out, the pillow was taken from under my head three times. When the bed rose up, it fell back without making any noise. This bed was so heavy, it took both the woman and the girl to pull it out from the wall without anybody in it, and there were only three castors on it."

The men tried sleeping in the other bed but it did them no good. "It kept very bad for the next few nights," Randall stated. "So Mr. Murphy, from the Guardian office, (the local police) and another man named Devereux, came and stopped in the room one night."

By now one of the lodgers, Richard, had given up and only two men remained, one sleeping in each of the two beds. In a signed statement Murphy and Devereux recorded how they carefully watched the evening's events from positions along the wall halfway between the two beds from which they could observe the entire room and the actions of both boarders.

"The night," wrote Murphy, "was a clear, starlight night. No blind obstructed the view from outside, and one could see the outlines of the beds and their occupants clearly. At about 11:30 a tapping was heard close at the foot of Randall's bed. My companion remarked that it appeared to be like the noise of a rat eating at timber.

"Sinnott replied, 'You'll soon see the rat it is.' The tapping went on slowly at first. Then the speed gradually increased to about a hundred or a hundred and twenty per minute, the noise growing louder. This continued for about five minutes, when it stopped suddenly. Randall then spoke. He said. 'The clothes are slipping off my bed. Look at them sliding off. Good God, they are going off me.'

"Mr. Devereux immediately struck a match, which he had ready in his hand. The bedclothes had partly left the boy's bed, having gone diagonally towards the foot, going out at the left corner, and not alone did they seem to be drawn off the bed, but they appeared to be actually going back under the bed, much in the same position one would expect bedclothes to be if a strong breeze were blowing through the room at the time. But then everything was perfectly calm."

The two investigators made a careful search for any wires or strings by which a fraud might have been perpetrated but found nothing. After the bedclothes were returned to his bed and the light was blown out, all was silent for about ten minutes.

Then Randall shouted that the bedclothes were beginning to slide off again. The investigators told him to try to hold on to them. Although he tried his best to comply, Randall soon cried out, "I'm going, I'm going, I'm gone!"

Upon striking a match, Randall, holding tight to the bedclothes, was seen to be sliding off the bed.

At this point, Sinnott had reached the limit of his endurance. Lying on the floor, violently trembling and soaked with perspiration, he cried, "I can't stand it! I can't stay here any longer!"

The poltergeist must have taken pity upon Sinnott because, after the investigators persuaded him to return to his bed, although more rapping was heard from another part of the room, eventually peace reigned for the remainder of the night.

No "normal" explanation was ever discovered for the ghostly phenomena and Murphy stated in his report, "Randall could not reach that part of the floor from which the rapping came on any occasion without attracting my attention and that of my comrade."

While I have long been of the opinion that what is termed a poltergeist is, more often than not, due to activity produced by what we traditionally think of as a ghost, I have recently begun to entertain the highly controversial possibility that, at least in some cases, there may be an even more curious explanation.

An Alternate Irish Theory

In Ireland poltergeist activity is often blamed on fairies retaliating against those who have build their houses upon paths said to be used by the fairies or upon those circular earthen mounds seen throughout Ireland known as "raths" or "fairy forts" in which the fairy folk are said to dwell. The fairy folk or "The Good People" or "The Gentry," as tradition informs us they prefer to be called, are not the delightfully charming, characters we have come to expect from fairy tales and Walt Disney films but they are, instead, entities which can, at times, be dangerous and who, when encountered, should be treated with the utmost caution and respect.

In times past it was common for those dwelling in areas in the Irish countryside known to be frequented by the fairies to, before retiring for the night, leave out offerings of small amounts of milk, butter, honey, stirabout or soda bread beside the hearth or outside the cottage door to insure a harmonious coexistence with "The Good People."

As recently as 1999, the route of a multi-million dollar motorway project in County Clare, Ireland was changed to curve round a whitethorn bush under which the fairies of Munster were said to rest and see to their wounds after engaging in fights with the fairies of Connaught. To remove the fairy bush which grew within path of the original route would, it was believed, incite the fairies to revenge and result in many accidents.

For centuries anyone wishing to build a new house anywhere in the countryside was well advised to check with the local "wise woman," a woman known to be knowledgeable concerning the "Otherworld," as to whether the proposed house site might intrude upon land claimed by the fairies or in any other way interfere with their activities. The historian Dermot MacManus records in his study of Irish supernatural entities, *The Middle Kingdom*, the fate of Paddy Blaine, one of his neighbors in Kiltimagh, County Mayo, Ireland, who failed to check with a wise woman before constructing his house. At night the house would sometimes shake so violently that he feared the house might tumble down upon him. He was advised to consult the local wise woman and, upon doing so, he learned that a corner of his house jutted out into a path the fairies often traveled and it needed to be removed. The offending corner of the house was removed and peace reigned in the house ever after.

In St. John D. Seymour and Harry L. Neligan's 1914 classic collection, *True Irish Ghost Stories*, the authors reported the following poltergeist incident which occurred in Portarlington, County Laos Ireland.

"A man near that town had saved five hundred pounds, and determined to build a house with the money. He fixed on a certain spot, and began to build, very much against the advice of his friends, who said it was on a fairy path, and would bring him ill-luck. Soon the house was finished, and the owner moved in; but the very first night his troubles began, for some unseen hand threw the furniture about and broke it, while the man himself was injured. Being unwilling to lose the value of his money, he tried to make the best of things. But night after night the disturbances continued, and life in the house was impossible; the owner chose the better part of valor and left. No tenant has been found since, and the house stands empty, a silent testimony to the power of the poltergeist."

As further evidence Seymour and Neligan presented the following correspondence regarding a man identified only as "Mr. M." who, previous to the events to be described, lived comfortably with his large family in a town in County Wexford, Ireland.

"Some twenty years ago," the correspondent wrote, "Mr. M., through the death of a relative, fell in for a legacy of about a hundred pounds. As he was already in rather prosperous circumstances, and as his old thatched dwelling house was not large enough to accommodate his increasing family, he resolved to spend the money in building a new one.

"Not long afterwards building operations commenced, and in about a year he had a fine slated cottage, or small farm-house, erected and ready for occupation.

"He purchased some new furniture at the nearest town, and on a certain day he removed all the furniture which the old house contained into the new one; and in the evening the family found themselves installed in the latter for good, as they thought. They all retired to rest at their usual hour; scarcely were they snugly settled in bed when they heard peculiar noises inside the house. As time passed the din became terrible — there was shuffling of feet, slamming of doors, pulling about of furniture, and so forth.

"The man of the house got up to explore, but could see nothing, neither was anything disturbed. The door was securely locked as he had left it. After a thorough investigation, in which his wife assisted, he had to own he could find no clue to the cause of the disturbance. The couple went to bed again, and almost immediately the racket recommenced, and continued more or less till dawn.

"The inmates were puzzled and frightened, but determined to try whether the noise would be repeated the next night before telling their neighbors what had happened. But the pandemonium experienced the first night of their occupation was as nothing compared with what they had to endure the second night and for several succeeding nights. Sleep was impossible, and finally Mr. M. and family in terror abandoned their new home, and retook possession of their old one.

"That is the state of things to this day. The old house has been repaired and is tenanted. The new house, a few perches off, facing the public road, is used as a storehouse. The writer has seen it scores of times, and its story is well known all over the countryside. Mr. M. is disinclined to discuss the matter or to answer questions; but it is said he made several subsequent attempts to occupy the house, but always failed to stand his ground when night came with its usual rowdy disturbances.

"It is said that when building operations were about to begin, a little man of bizarre appearance accosted Mr. M. and exhorted him to build on a different site; otherwise the consequences would be unpleasant for him and his; while the local peasantry allege that the house was built across a fairy pathway between two raths and that this was the cause of the trouble. It is quite true that there are two large raths in the vicinity, and the haunted house is directly in a bee-line between them. For myself I offer no explanation; but I guarantee the substantial accuracy of what I have stated above."

Ghostly Imprints

Some parapsychologists feel that ghosts are merely psychic echoes of the past. They suggest that incidents from the past, particularly violent or highly emotional events, can sometimes imprint themselves into the rooms or landscape in which these incidents had occurred, becoming an indelible part of the atmosphere — psychic imprints replaying themselves over and over again, unnoticed by all but those who are in a state of mind conducive to seeing or hearing them.

Examples of what I believe to be psychic imprints can be found at the previously cited Holbrooke Hotel where late at night, when its Golden Gate Saloon is locked up tight and hotel guests are fast asleep in their rooms, the voices of revelers from another era can sometimes be heard emanating from within the Saloon and where, in broad daylight, a young boy once complained of hearing loud voices issuing forth from the adjacent room, a room which was, at the time, completely empty.

Just a few blocks away on Mill Street, gun shots have, on a number of occasions, been heard to ring out from within a building in which, long ago, it is said that a man was shot to death behind the iron doors near the rear of the building. And, then, there is the piano music and the sound of dancing which has been heard coming from the building's completely empty and unoccupied second floor.

The Battle of Edge Hill

Perhaps the most dramatic examples of such phenomena involve phantom battles which have, on occasion, been observed on historic battlefields in which the conflict is reenacted, over and over again by ghostly combatants.

On October 23, 1642 the Parliamentarians fought the Royalists at Edge Hill in Warwickshire, England in what would be the first major battle of the English Civil War. By the end of the day, the blood-soaked battle field was awash with corpses and what one Royalist decried as "200 miserable maimed solders, without relief of money or surgeons, horribly crying out upon the villainy of those men who corrupted them."

Weeks later rumors of phantom armies reenacting the battle reached the ears of King Charles I and he sent a Royal Commission of six of his most trusted military officers to Edge Hill to investigate the stories and to "report upon these prodigies, and to tranquillize and disabuse the alarms of a country town."

"On Saturday, which was in Christmas time" wrote the Commission members in their report back to the King, "between twelve and one of the clock in the morning, was heard by some shepherds first the sound of drums afar off and the noise of soldiers giving out their last groans; at which they were much amazed, and amazed stood still, till it seemed by the nearness of the noise to approach them; at which, too much affrighted, they sought to withdraw as fast as possibly they could."

But, before the shepherds could flee, the sky was filled with "strange and portentous apparitions of two jarring and contrary armies — the same incorporeal soldiers that made those clamors, the clattering of arms, noise of cannons, ensigns displayed, drums beating, muskets going off, cannons discharged, horses neighing, cries of soldiers, and the two armies — pell-mell to it they went. So amazing and terrifying the poor men, that they could not believe they were mortal, or give credit to their eyes and ears; run away they durst not, for fear of being made a prey to these infernal soldiers, and so they, with much fear and affright, stayed to behold the success of the business."

The phantom battle continued for three hours, at which point the ghostly armies dissolved into the night air and "The shepherds made haste to Kineton, where they woke up Mr. Wood, a Justice of Peace, and his neighbor, Mr. Marshall, the Minister."

"The following night," the Commission's report continues, "all the substantial inhabitants of that and the neighboring parishes drew thither; where, about half an hour after their arrival, on Sunday, being Christmas night, appeared in the same tumultuous warlike manner, the same two adverse armies, fighting with as much spite and spleen as formerly; and so departed the gentlemen and all the spectators, much terrified with these visions of horror, withdrew themselves to their houses, beseeching God to defend them from those hellish and prodigious enemies."

When the Royal Commission arrived at Edge Hill, the ghostly reenactment was still occurring at night and they, officers who, themselves, had taken part in the battle, were amazed to see it all unfold before them exactly as they had seen it on the day of the battle. In particular, they described observing the death of the King's standard bearer, Sir Edmund Verney, his hand so firmly clutching the Royal Standard that the Parliamentarians had to chop it off.

Strangest of all, members of the Commission observed Prince Rupert, a Royalist commander, in the midst of the phantom battle although he had survived the battle and he would go on to live for another forty years!

Although all of this occurred hundreds of years ago, from time to time, modern reports are still made of witnesses hearing the roar of cannons, the screams of long-dead soldiers and the clash of steel upon steel at Edge Hill, especially during the month of October.

Similar phantom battles have been reported over the years at Gettysburg, Sharpsburg and other battlefields from the American Civil War.

Animal Ghosts

Do animals have spirits which survive death? Might we someday be reunited with pets which have passed on before us? Numerous first-hand accounts suggest that this is more likely than not the case. And it is equally likely that our animal friends are far more in touch with the world of spirits than we are.

Phantom Dogs

Typical of accounts concerning dogs which remain with their owners past the time of their death as well as their sensitivity to ghosts is the following letter which I received in 1977 from a lady by the name of Edith Southern.

"A few years ago my fourteen-year-old daughter, our dog, Lassie, and I were going up Link road here in Winston-Salem. It was around 10:30 p.m. We were going to get her horse so she could ride him the next day. It was moonless and quiet. As we were rounding a curve with just a streetlight across the street from us, I looked down the embankment and there stood a young man dressed in a dark suit a white shirt and a dark tie. I could feel that he was friendly and meant us no harm. Lassie kept growling at him and the hair stood raised up and down her back (she was a smooth collie.) I told her to be quiet for I could feel friendly emanations coming from the young man and I felt no fear. He stood watching us as we came around a curve, there in the full light from the street lamp, and just a few feet from where I was walking. Sudden chills ran up my back. The little boy did not have a head! His body ended at the shoulders. My daughter was up ahead and Lassie took off running and so did I.

"I caught up with my daughter and she said 'Mother, he didn't have a head!' That erased any doubts that could have arisen for my daughter, the dog and I knew he was there. We never walked that road again, believe me.

"We kept Lassie for ten and a half years until she died. She was only afraid of thunder storms. For years after she died whenever there were thunder storms she would come into my bedroom, her nails clicking on the wooden floors and, with a sigh, ease her heavy body on the floor beside my bed, and I would tell her 'It's all right it will be over soon.'

"Four years ago I had a toy poodle. When he was eight months old he was killed by the German shepherd next door. Every night he would get frightened when we would go to bed and run and jump up on the foot of my bed. This still, ever so often, after being dead for nearly three years, I feel him jump on my bed and turn around and around till he found a place to curl up and sleep."

The Black Retriever

In a first-hand account written and signed by the witness, James Durham, we have the case of a phantom dog which remained with and protected his equally phantom master. This case is particularly strong as it was investigated by Edward Pease, remembered in England as the "Father of Railways."

"I was night watchman at the old Darlington and Stockton Station at the town of Darlington," wrote Durham, "a few yards from the first station that ever existed. I was there fifteen years. I used to go on duty about 8 p.m. and come off at 6 a.m.

"One night during winter at about twelve o'clock or twelve-thirty I was feeling rather cold with standing here and there; I said to myself, 'I will away down and get something to eat.' There was a porter's cellar where a fire was kept on and a coal-house was connected with it. So I went down the steps, took off my overcoat, and had just sat down on the bench opposite the fire and turned up the gas when a strange man came out of the coal-house, followed by a big black retriever. As soon as he entered my eye was upon him, and his eye upon me, and we were intently watching each other as he moved on to the front of the fire. There he stood looking at me, and a curious smile came over his countenance. He had a stand-up collar and a cutaway coat with gilt buttons and a Scotch cap.

"All at once he struck at me, and I had the impression that he hit me. I up with my fist and struck back at him. My fist seemed to go through him and struck against the stone above the fireplace, and knocked the skin off my knuckles. The man seemed to be struck back into the fire, and uttered a strange, unearthly squeak. Immediately the dog gripped me by the calf of my leg, and seemed to cause me pain. The man recovered his position, called off the dog with a sort of click of the tongue, then went back into the coal-house, followed by the dog. I lighted my dark lantern and looked into the coal-house, but there was neither dog nor man, and no outlet for them except the one by which they had entered.

"I was satisfied that what I had seen was ghostly, and it accounted for the fact that when the man had first come into the place where he sat I had not challenged him with any enquiry.

"Next day, and for several weeks, my account caused quite a commotion, and a host of people spoke to me about it; among the rest old Edward

Pease, Father of Railways, and his three sons, John, Joseph, and Henry. Old Edward sent for me to his house and asked me all particulars. He and others put this question to me: 'Are you sure you were not asleep and had the nightmare?' My answer was quite sure, for I had not been a minute in the cellar, and was just going to get something to eat. I was certainly not under the influence of strong drink, for I was then, as I have been for forty-nine years, a teetotaler. My mind at the time was perfectly free from trouble.

"What increased the excitement was the fact that a man a number of years before, who was employed in the office of the station, had committed suicide, and his body had been carried into this very cellar. I knew nothing of this circumstance, nor of the body of the man, but Mr. Pease and others who had known him, told me my description exactly corresponded to his appearance and the way he dressed, and also that he had a black retriever just like the one which gripped me.

"I should add that no mark or effect remained on the spot where I seemed to be seized."

The majority of animal ghosts reported to the Society for Psychical research were dogs or cats. Among these accounts were the following three cases involving phantom cats.

Smokey

"My sister, H. L. Green, had a very favorite cat called Smoky, a pure-bred blue Persian of peculiar shade and small. There was no other cat in the village in the least like her. In the spring she became ill and died about the middle of June 1909. The gardener buried her, and planted a dahlia over her grave. Shortly before Smoky died she had been worried by a dog, and had her ribs broken, so that she walked quite lame. This injury was the final cause of her death.

"On Tuesday, July 6th, 1909, my sister and I were at breakfast, and I was reading a letter aloud to her. I was sitting with my back to the window, which was on my sister's left. Suddenly I saw her looking absolutely scared, and gazing out of the window. I said, 'What is the matter?' and she said, 'There's Smoky, walking across the grass!' We both rushed to the window, and saw Smoky, looking very ill, her coat rough and staring, and walking lamely across the grass in front of the window, three or four yards from it.

"My sister called her, and as she took no notice, she ran out after her, calling her. I remained at the window, and saw the cat turn down a path leading to the end of the garden. My sister ran after her, calling her, but to her surprise, Smoky did not turn or take any notice, and she lost sight of her among the shrubs.

"About ten minutes afterwards, my sister and a friend living with us saw Smoky again going through a hedge in front of the window. My sister again went out after her, but could not find her.

"She was next seen about half an hour afterwards by the servant, in the kitchen passage. She ran to get her some milk and followed her with it, but the cat walked away, and from that moment she disappeared completely. We made every inquiry of the neighbors, but no one had seen her, or any cat like her.

"Of course we thought there had been some mistake about her death, though our friend the gardener and the boy had all seen her dead. The gardener was so indignant at the suspicion that he had not buried the cat that he went to the grave, took up the plant, and dug up the body of Smoky.

"We are quite mystified at the occurrence, which was witnessed by four people, namely B. J. Green, H. L. Green, Miss Smith, and Kathleen B. (servant).

"When last seen the cat was walking towards the house, next door, where she had lived all the winter and spring. But when my sister went over there, the people at the house had seen nothing of her. When my sister first ran out after her, the cat ran away in front of her, moving fast, but on one side, as she did before she died."

The Persistent Feline

While seeing a phantom cat is highly unusual, one which follows a family from one residence to another is nothing short of extraordinary. On December 14th, 1890, a Mrs. Erni Greiffenberg wrote:

"In the beginning of the summer of 1884 we were sitting at dinner at home as usual, in the middle of the day. In the midst of the conversation I noticed my mother suddenly looking down at something beneath the table. I inquired whether she had dropped anything, and received the answer, 'No, but I wonder how that cat can have got into the room?' Looking underneath the table, I was surprised to see a large white Angora cat beside my mother's chair. We both got up, and I opened the door to let the cat out. She marched round the table, went noiselessly out of the door, and when about half way down the passage turned round and faced us. For a short time she regularly stared at us with her green eyes, and then she dissolved away, like a mist, under our eyes.

"Even apart from the mode of her disappearance, we felt convinced that the cat could not have been a real one, as we neither had one of our own, nor knew of any that would answer to the description in the place, and so this appearance made an unpleasant impression upon us.

"This impression was, however, greatly enhanced by what happened in the following year, 1885, when we were staying in Leipzig with my married sister (the daughter of Mrs. Greiffenberg.) We had come home one afternoon from a walk, when on opening the door of the flat, we were met in the hall by the same white cat. It proceeded down the passage in front of us, and looked at us with the same melancholy gaze. When it got to the door of the cellar (which was locked), it again dissolved into nothing.

"On this occasion also it was first seen by my mother, and we were both impressed by the uncanny and gruesome character of the appearance. In this case, also, the cat could not have been a real one, as there was no such cat in the neighborhood.

The Cat's Revenge

While it might be argued that the grief resulting from the loss of a much loved pet might cause a distressed owner to hallucinate or to misinterpret natural phenomena as an indication of their pet's survival past death, such a possibility could hardly explain the following account submitted by a Mrs. Gordon Jones in 1892.

"I have the strongest aversion to cats" she wrote, "— a tendency which I have inherited from my father, who could not endure a cat's presence. After my marriage, I would never have one in the house, until obliged to do so on account of mice. The one that I then allowed to come was an ordinary grey and black striped one — but I very seldom looked at it, and it was never allowed to come upstairs.

"One day I was told that the cat was mad and asked if it might be drowned. I did not look at the animal myself, but said, 'Yes.' I next heard that it had been drowned by the groom in a copper. As the cat was not a pet and had never been my companion, its death made no impression on me.

"It was drowned in the morning. The same evening I was sitting alone in the dining-room. I am sure that I was not thinking of the cat or of possible apparitions. I was reading; presently I felt impelled to look up, the door seemed to open, and there stood the animal that had been drowned in the morning; the same cat, but apparently much thinner and dripping with water — only the expression of the face was changed — the eyes were quite human and haunted me afterwards, they looked so sad and pathetic. I felt so sure of what I saw that at the moment I never doubted that it was the living cat who had escaped from drowning.

"I rang the bell and when the servant came I said, 'There's the cat, take it out,' it seemed to me that she could not but see it too — it was clear and distinct to my eyes as the table or chairs. But the servant looked frightened and said, 'Oh, ma'am, I saw the cat after William had drowned it — and then he buried it in the garden.' 'But', I said, 'there it is.' Of course she saw nothing, and then the cat began to fade, and I saw nothing more of it."

Thought-Forms

Many parapsychologists theorize that ghosts are merely the result of a telepathic hallucination. The idea is that, in a moment of extreme emotionality, a living person concentrates so intensely upon the event he or she is experiencing that it creates a "thought-form" which resides indefinitely within the place in which it was created or in a place, perhaps hundreds of miles away, about which the person who created it was thinking at the time it was created.

This thought-form is, then, telepathically received as a hallucination, either at the moment of its creation or sometime later, perhaps even many years later, by one or more persons who are, at that time, in a state of mind conducive to receiving telepathic images and who are present in the place in which the though-form resides.

While this theory makes sense in cases of what appear to be imprint ghosts, I personally feel it is inadequate to fully explain apparitions which appear to demonstrate a functioning consciousness and the ability to interact with the living.

However, while it may seem impossible that a ghost could be accidentally created through the sheer power of one's mind, we do have cases on record which suggest that one might be consciously created.

The Philip Experiment

In 1972 an extraordinarily creative experiment was carried out in Canada by the Toronto Society for Psychical Research under the direction of the mathematical geneticist, Dr. A. R. George Owen. Their goal was to see if they could produce ghost-like manifestations through the creation of an entirely fictitious entity.

Their first step was to write a fictional biography for their completely imaginary ghost whom they named Philip Aylesford; a biography which reads like a historical romance novel.

Philip, they decided, was an aristocrat and a Royalist during the time of the English Civil War. Knighted at the age of sixteen and a close friend of Charles II, he served during the war as a spy.

Unfortunately, Philip was trapped in a loveless marriage to the beautiful but cold, cruel and violent Dorothea. As Philip was a Roman Catholic, divorce was impossible.

One day, while riding through the outermost regions of his domain, Philip chanced upon a Romani camp where he encountered Margo, an enchanting dark-haired beauty with hypnotic blue eyes which Philip felt could see into the depths of his soul. It was "love at first sight" and soon Philip had Margo secretly ensconced in the gatehouse of his home, Diddington Manor.

When Dorothea eventually learned of her husband's "love nest," she accused Margot of employing witchcraft to steal her husband. Afraid of sullying his reputation, Philip failed to come to his lover's defence and Margo was burned alive at the stake.

One morning, consumed by guilt, Philip ended his life at the age of thirty by hurling himself from the battlements of his castle.

The group even had a portrait drawn of their imaginary ghost.

For approximately a year, eight members of the group conducted a series of weekly meetings in which, in a fully lit room, they spoke of the details of Philip's life and meditated on these details in the hope of creating a collective hallucination. Although some members of the group reported feeling a "presence" having drawn near them, nothing of any real consequence occurred.

Their initial plan having failed, the group decided to try a different approach, an old-fashioned séance along the lines of those practiced by nineteenth century spiritualists. They dimmed the lights, sat around a card table, sang songs and surrounded themselves with pictures of the kind of castle in which Philip might have lived as well as other objects with which Philip would have been familiar. And, placing their fingers upon the table, they called out for Philip to make is presence known to them.

During the fourth session in which they employed this technique, without warning, they began to feel the table vibrate beneath their fingertips and a loud rap was heard issuing from somewhere within the table. Utilizing the traditional code of one rap for "Yes" and two raps for "No," they asked Philip a series of questions about his life, all of which were answered by raps which accurately matched both his fictional biography and historical facts regarding life in England during the mid-seventeenth century.

In the sessions which followed, the group reported the table tipping and, then, gliding across the floor. Philip was alleged to have, at times, controlled the lights and even to have whispered answers to their questions.

During the next four years, they invited witnesses to observe their séance sessions and even successfully produced the phenomena under the scrutiny of television lights and cameras.

By the fifth year, however, they ended the experiment, as Dr. Owens felt that they were clearly unable to achieve their ultimate objective, the production of a visible apparition.

The Toronto group's experiment had been inspired by an account in which, if true, a visible apparition had been created solely though the power of the mind.

The Tulpa

In her 1929 book, *Magic and Mystery in Tibet*, the French singer and adventurer, Alexandra David-Néel, wrote of the "tulpa," a Tibetan phantom which she claimed may be created "by the power generated in a state of perfect concentration of mind."

Having encountered a tupla on at least three previous occasions while in Tibet, Madam David-Néel decided to attempt to create a tupla for herself.

She chose for her experiment "a monk, short and fat, of an innocent and jolly type."

Going into an extended period of seclusion, she performed "the prescribed concentration of thought and other rites." Within a few months, the tulpa was gradually formed and it lived with her in her apartment.

When she ended her period of seclusion and, again, began to travel for miles each day with her retinue of servants, tents and other supplies, Madame David- Néel observed that the tulpa followed along with her. And at least one other person, a herdsman who brought her a gift of butter, saw the tulpa so clearly that he mistakenly thought it to be a living person.

But, then, the tupla's appearance began to change. "The fat, chubby-cheeked fellow grew leaner," she wrote, "his face assumed a vaguely mocking, sly, malignant look. He became more troublesome and bold. In brief, he escaped my control."

This change in the tupla's appearance and behavior began to frighten her and the experiment became for her a nightmare. She decided to destroy the phantom she had created, an extremely difficult task which took over six months. "My mind-creature," she wrote, "was tenacious of life."

Perhaps the great Irish playwright, Bernard Shaw, was more insightful than he knew when he wrote, "Imagination is the beginning of creation. You imagine what you desire, you will what you imagine and at last you create what you will."

The Cheltenham Ghost

When a haunting is recorded by a highly intelligent, daring and thoughtful witness and it is carefully investigated by a distinguished officer of the Society for Psychical Research, we have an example of paranormal phenomena which should give even the most hardened skeptic cause to reconsider his beliefs. Such is the case of the Cheltenham ghost.

Around the year of 1860, a fine three-story residence was constructed on Pittville Circus Road in Cheltenham, England upon the former site of a market garden. It was bought by Henry Swinhoe, an Anglo-Indian gentleman who lived there for sixteen years with his wife, Elisabeth, to whom he was passionately devoted, and their young children. Then tragedy struck. Mrs. Swinhoe died and her husband attempted to escape his grief through heavy drinking.

Around two years later Mr. Swinhoe married a woman named Imogen. Although Imogen initially had hopes of curtailing her husband's drinking, she became dependent upon alcohol as well with the result that the marriage was the scene of continuous quarreling and marital violence. The arguments revolved mainly around the discipline of the children of his first marriage and Imogen's desire to possess his first wife's jewelry. Disputes over the jewelry became so heated that, in an effort to save the jewelry for his daughters, Mr. Swinhoe had a carpenter pull up some floorboards in the front sitting room and create beneath them a small box in which the jewelry could be safely hidden from his wife.

On July 14th, 1876, Henry Swinhoe died. Imogen, who had already left Henry and moved to Clifton a few months before, died on September 23rd, 1878 and, although it is believed that she never returned to the house in life, she was buried in the churchyard of Holy Trinity Church only a quarter of a mile from the house.

The house was next occupied by an elderly couple who lived there until, six months after moving in, the husband died. The house was then to remain unoccupied for approximately four years. During this time a gardener was said to have often seen a tall woman in black in the garden and a lady who had once lived in the area later reported seeing a woman fitting that same description inside the house.

The house was next rented by Captain Frederick W. Despard who, at the end of April, 1882, moved into the house with his family consisting of his invalid wife, Harriet; four daughters, then aged nineteen, eighteen, fifteen and thirteen; two sons, aged sixteen and six and three servants. A married daughter, age twenty-six, was often a visitor to the house.

It was the nineteen year old daughter, Rosina Clara Despard, to whom we are indebted for recording what is was is, perhaps, the most complete account of a haunting on record; an account which was carefully investigated and deemed to be authentic by Frederic W. H. Myers, a founding member of the Society for Psychical Research. Highly intelligent and possessing a keen scientific mind, Rosina would, in 1895, receive a medical degree from the London School of Medicine, a highly unusual accomplishment at a time when very few women were allowed into the profession; Rosina being only the twenty-third woman to receive a medical degree.

A little more than a month after her family had moved into the house, Rosina experienced her first ghostly encounter.

"I had gone up to my room," she wrote, "but was not yet in bed, when I heard someone at the door and went to it, thinking it might be my mother. On opening the door, I saw no one; but on going a few steps along the passage, I saw the figure of a tall lady, dressed in black, standing at the head of the stairs. After a few moments she descended the stairs and I followed for a short distance, feeling curious what it could be. I had only a small piece of candle and it suddenly burnt itself out; and, being unable to see more, I went back to my room.

"The figure was that of a tall lady, dressed in black of a soft woolen material, judging from the slight sound in moving. The face was hidden in a handkerchief held in the right hand. This is all I noticed then; but on further occasions, when I was able to observe her more closely, I saw the upper part of the left side of the forehead and a little of the hair above. Her left hand was nearly hidden by her sleeve and a fold of her dress. As she held it down a portion of a widow's cuff was visible on both wrists, so that the whole impression was that of a lady in widow's weeds. There was no cap on the head but a general effect of blackness suggests a bonnet, with long veil or a hood.

"During the next two years — from 1882 to 1884 — I saw the figure about half a dozen times; at first at long intervals and afterwards at shorter but I only mentioned these appearances to one friend, who did not speak of them to anyone.

"After the first time, I followed the figure several times downstairs into the drawing-room, where she remained a variable time, generally standing to the right hand side of the bow window. From the drawing-room she went along the passage towards the garden door, where she always disappeared.

"During this period, as far as we know, there were only three appearances to anyone else."

In the summer of 1882 Rosina's married sister, Freda, saw the woman. While coming down the staircase to dinner, she saw what she thought to be a nun visiting the house cross in front of her and enter the drawing-room. "Who was that Sister of Mercy whom I have just seen going into the drawing room?" she asked members of her family who were already assembled at the dinner table. No one at the table knew of any visitors and, when a servant was dispatched to look, she reported that no one was in the drawing room and no visitors had entered the house. Still Freda was adamant that she had seen "a tall figure in black, with some white about it."

It was in autumn of the following year that a servant reported seeing a woman matching the same description at around 10 p.m. but, as a search of the house revealed no intruder, the servant was not believed.

Then, on or about December 18th, 1883, the woman was seen in the drawing room by Rosina's youngest brother and another young boy. "They were playing outside on the terrace," Rosina wrote, "when they saw the figure in the drawing-room close to the window and ran in to see who it could be that was crying so bitterly. They found no one in the drawing-room and the parlor maid told them that no one had come into the house."

On 29th of January Rosina fearlessly attempted to speak to the phantom. "I opened the drawing-room door softly" she recorded, "and went in, standing just by it. She came in past me and walked to the sofa and stood still there. So I went up to her and asked her if I could help her. She moved and I thought she was going to speak, but she only gave a slight gasp and moved towards the door. Just by the door I spoke to her again but she seemed as if she were quite unable to speak. She walked into the hall, then by the side door she seemed to disappear as before.

"I also attempted to touch her, but she always eluded me. It was not that there was nothing there to touch but that she always seemed to be beyond me and if followed into a corner, simply disappeared.

"As to the feelings aroused by the presence of the figure, it is very difficult to describe them; on the first few occasions, I think the feeling of awe at something unknown, mixed with a strong desire to know more about it, predominated. Later, when I was able to analyze my feelings more closely and the first novelty had gone off, I felt conscious of a feeling of loss, as if I had lost power to the figure.

"In May and June, 1884, I tried some experiments, fastening strings with marine glue across the stairs before going to bed but after all others have gone up to their rooms. I made small pellets of marine glue, into which I inserted the ends of the cord, then stuck one pellet lightly against the wall and the other to the banister, the string being thus stretched across the stairs. They were knocked down by a very slight touch and yet would not be felt by anyone passing up or down the stairs and by candle-light could not be seen from below. They were put at various heights from the ground, from six inches to the height of the banisters, about three feet. I have twice at least seen the figure pass through the cords, leaving them intact."

During the next two months, July and August, 1884, sightings of the lady in black became much more frequent. Rosina states that during these months the haunting was at its maximum.

"On July 31st, sometime after I had gone up to bed, my second sister Edith, who had remained downstairs talking in another sister's room, came to me saying that someone had passed her on the stairs. I tried then to persuade her that it was one of the servants but next morning found it could not have been so, as none of them had been out of their rooms at that hour and Edith's more detailed description tallied with what I had already seen.

"On the night of August 1st, I again saw the figure. I heard the footsteps outside on the landing about 2 a.m. I got up at once and went outside. She was then at the end of the landing at the top of the stairs, with her side view towards me. She stood there some minutes, then went downstairs, stopping again when she reached the hall below. I opened the drawing-room door and she went in, walked across the room to the couch in the bow window, stayed there a little, then came out of the room, went along the passage, and disappeared by the garden door. I spoke to her again but she did not answer.

"On the night of August 2nd the footsteps were heard by my three sisters and by the cook, all of whom slept on the top landing; also by my married sister who was sleeping on the floor below. They all said the next morning that they had heard them very plainly pass and repass their doors. These footsteps are very characteristic and are not at all like those of any of the people in the house; they are soft and rather slow, though decided and even. Her footstep is very light, you can hardly hear it, except on the linoleum and then only like a person walking softly with thin boots on. My sisters would not go out on the landing after hearing them pass, nor would the servants, but each time when I have gone out after hearing them, I have seen the figure there.

"The cook was a middle-aged and very sensible person; on my asking her the following morning if any of the servants had been out of their rooms the night before, after coming up to bed, she told me that she had heard these footsteps before and that she had seen the figure on the stairs one night when going down to the kitchen to fetch hot water after the servants had come up to bed. She described it as a lady in widow's dress, tall and slight, with her face hidden in a handkerchief held in her right hand. She also saw the figure outside the kitchen windows on the terrace-walk, she herself being in the kitchen; it was then about eleven in the morning.

"On August 12th, about 8 p.m., and still quite light, my sister Edith was singing in the back drawing-room. I heard her stop abruptly, come out into the hall and call me. She said she had seen the figure in the drawing-room, close behind her as she sat at the piano. I went back into the room with her and saw the figure in the bow window in her usual place. I spoke to her several times, but had no answer. She stood there for about ten minutes or a quarter of an hour; then went across the room to the door, and along the passage, disappearing in the same place by the garden door."

At this point Rosina's youngest sister came into the house from the garden to tell them that she had seen the ghost moving up the outside kitchen steps. No sooner had the three sisters left the house and entered the garden than Freda called to them from a first storey window to tell them that she had just seen the ghost "pass across the lawn in front, and along the carriage drive towards the orchard." That evening four people had each seen the ghost from four different vantage points.

During this period the ghost was not only seen by family members but also by a retired general living across the street, a gardener, their parlor maid and a charwoman.

Even their two dogs seemed aware of the ghost. "A retriever who slept in the kitchen was on several occasions found by the cook in a state of terror, when she went into the kitchen in the morning," Rosina recalled. "Being a large dog, he was not allowed upstairs; he was also seen more than once coming from the orchard thoroughly cowed and terrified. He was kindly treated and not at all a nervous dog.

"A small Skye Terrier, whom we had later, was allowed about the house; he usually slept on my bed and undoubtedly heard the footsteps outside the door. On October 27th, 1887 the dog was then suffering from an attack of rheumatism and very disinclined to move but on hearing the footsteps it sprang up and sniffed at the door. Twice I remember seeing this dog suddenly run up to the mat at the foot of the stairs in the hall, wagging its tail, and moving its back in the way dogs do when expecting to be caressed. It jumped up, fawning as it would do if a person had been standing there, but suddenly slunk away with its tail between its legs, and retreated, trembling, under a sofa. We were all strongly under the impression that it had seen the figure. Its action was peculiar and was much more striking to an onlooker than it could possibly appear from a description."

The cat, however, which usually stayed only in the kitchen seemed to be completely unaware of anything of a supernatural nature.

Following the events of July and August, 1884, the sightings and ghostly sounds gradually began to decline in frequency until, eventually, they seem to have ended.

Captain Despard made inquires as to the history of the House and found several people who identified the ghost from Rosina's description as being Imogen Swinhoe, an identification which made sense to Rosina due to the ghost being dressed in widow's weeds and the fact that the second Mrs. Swinhoe was the only person associated with the house who in anyway resembled the ghost. Upon being shown an album containing a number of photographic portraits, Rosina picked out a photograph of Imogen Swinhoe's sister as being most like that of the ghost she had seen so often and "was afterwards told that the sisters were much alike."

Critics have theorized that the lady in black might have been a mistress of Captain Despard attempting to leave the house after clandestine rendezvous, pointing out that the woman's face was observed to be hidden by the handkerchief held in her right hand. Such an explanation, however, ignores the fact that the same figure had been observed in the house during the years prior to the Despard's occupancy and the fact that she was seen to pass through solid objects and to inexplicably disappear when cornered.

As time went on, the ghost gradually became less visually distinct in appearance. However light footsteps were heard throughout the house as late as 1892 and the lady in black was seen several times in the front garden in 1903.

The house, which still stands on Pittville Circus Road, was, at a later time, utilized as a private school but the school was forced to close due to what was described as "constant trouble from the ghost." Finally, it was turned into a block of apartments. A Mr. Thorne, a tenant residing in one of the apartments from 1957 to 1962 reported often seeing and hearing the ghost.

The Doppelganger

Have you ever had the eerie experience of clearly recognizing someone on the street whom you knew, without a doubt, could not be there as he was miles away at the time. Or, even more disturbing, have you ever come face to face with your own double? If so, you may have encountered the doppelganger. Known as the "Wraith" in Scotland, the "Fetch" in Ireland, the etheric double and by numerous other names throughout the world, the doppelganger is, perhaps, the most perplexing of all apparitions.

The Black Bordered Letter

"On January the 23rd or 24th, 1881, between two or three in the afternoon, I saw an apparition of the living when I was ill in bed at my own home," wrote the witness. "There was in the room a nurse seated at the fire. We had been quite quiet, but I had not been sleeping. I saw my husband come into the room in a very quick and agitated manner. His face was white, and the features were twitching. He came right up to my side, and stood by me, looking at me earnestly. He was dressed in his ordinary clothes, his hat was off, and I had not the least idea that it was not his ordinary self. He had in one hand a letter, with a very broad black border, torn open.

"I waited for him to speak; instead of doing so, he suddenly turned and went away, I did not see him go out of the door. When I realized that he was gone I called him, saying, 'Come back; what is the matter?'

"The nurse turned and said, 'What is it? Do you want anything?'

"I said that I wanted my husband to return and to tell me what was in the letter.

"She said, 'You have been dreaming. There has been nobody in the room.'

"I answered, 'You have been asleep. My husband has just been here, and he has a letter containing bad news.'

"I insisted upon her going down and asking him to come back. She did not return for about a quarter of an hour. Then she said, no one had been in the room, so I must have been dreaming. I was to calm myself, and my husband would come presently. Nothing would induce me to believe that I had not really seen him, and I was too weak to be calm. I begged her to go down again, and my husband's sister came upstairs. She said, 'He has not been upstairs at all.

You have been dreaming.' She laughed, and tried to put me at my ease, but her manner was unnatural.

"My husband did not come up for quite three hours, when he declared that he had not been in the room; that at the time I saw him he was, as a matter of fact, out of the house, and that the postman had not been to the house that afternoon. I was obliged to be contented for the time.

"A fortnight later, when I was stronger and up, I asked him to tell me the truth. I was certain that I had been in some way deceived. He said it was absolutely true that he had been out, and that the postman had not come, but the groom had met the postman, and given my husband the black-edged letter that I saw, which he had torn open in the way I saw, and it contained the news of the suicide by hanging of a favorite cousin, who had been a playfellow of my husband's when a child. When he received this shock, I received it too."

A Protective Double

And then there is the case of a professor at a college at Berlin, who, as preserved by Catherine Crowe in *The Night Side of Nature*, one day "addressed his class, saying, that, instead of his usual lecture, he should relate to them a circumstance which, the preceding evening, had occurred to himself.

"He then told them," wrote Miss Crowe, "that, as he was going home the last evening, he had seen his own image, or double, on the other side of the street. He looked away, and tried to avoid it, but, finding it still accompanied him, he took a shortcut home, in hopes of getting rid of it, wherein he succeeded, till he came opposite his own house, when he saw it (the double) at the door. It rang, the maid opened, it entered, she handed it a candle, and, as the professor stood in amazement, on the other side of the street, he saw the light passing the windows, as it wound its way up to his own chamber.

"He (the professor) then crossed over and rang; the servant was naturally dreadfully alarmed on seeing him, but, without waiting to explain, he ascended the stairs. Just as he reached his own chamber, he heard a loud crash, and, on opening the door, they found no one there, but the ceiling had fallen in, and his life was thus saved.

"The servant corroborated this statement to the students."

The Surgeon's Apprentice

An even more intriguing case involving a doppelganger occurred in the late 1700's.

"The apprentice, or assistant, of a respectable surgeon in Glasgow," wrote Miss Crowe, "was known to have had an illicit connection with a servant-girl, who somewhat suddenly disappeared. No suspicion, however, seems to have been entertained of foul play. It appears rather to have been supposed that she had retired for the purpose of being confined, and, consequently, no inquiries were made about her.

"Glasgow was, at that period, a very different place to what it is at present, in more respects than one; and, among its peculiarities, was the extraordinary strictness with which the observance of the Sabbath was enforced, insomuch, that nobody was permitted to show themselves in the streets or public walks during the hours dedicated to the church services; and there were actually inspectors appointed to see that this regulation was observed, and to take down the names of defaulters.

"At one extremity of the city, there is some open ground, of rather considerable extent, on the north side of the river, called 'The Green,' where people sometimes resort for air and exercise; and where lovers not infrequently retire to enjoy as much solitude as the proximity to so large a town can afford.

"One Sunday morning, the inspectors of public piety above alluded to having traversed the city, and extended their perquisitions as far as the lower extremity of the Green, where it was bounded by a wall, observed a young man lying on the grass, whom they immediately recognized to be the surgeon's assistant. They, of course, inquired why he was not at church, and proceeded to register his name in their books, but, instead of attempting to make any excuse for his offence, he only rose from the ground, saying, 'I am a miserable man. Look in the water!' He then immediately crossed a stile, which divided the wall, and led to a path extending along the side of the river toward the Rutherglen road. They saw him cross the stile, but, not comprehending the significance of his words, instead of observing him further, they naturally directed their attention to the water, where they presently perceived the body of a woman.

"Having with some difficulty dragged it ashore, they immediately proceeded to carry it into the town, assisted by several other persons, who by this time had joined them. It was now about one o'clock, and, as they passed through the streets, they were obstructed by the congregation that was issuing from one of the principal places of worship; and, as they stood up for a moment, to let them pass, they saw the surgeon's assistant issue from the church door. As it was quite possible for him to have gone round some other way, and got there before them, they were not much surprised. He did not approach them, but mingled with the crowd, while they proceeded on their way.

"On examination, the woman proved to be the missing servant-girl. She was pregnant, and had evidently been murdered with a surgeon's instrument, which was found entangled among her clothes. Upon this, in consequence of his known connection with her, and his implied self-accusation to the inspectors, the young man was apprehended on suspicion of being the guilty party, and tried upon the circuit. He was the last person seen in her company, immediately previous to her disappearance; and there was, altogether, such strong presumptive evidence against him, as corroborated by what occurred on the green would have justified a verdict of guilty. But, strange to say, this last most important item in the evidence failed, and he established an incontrovertible alibi; it being proved, beyond all possibility of doubt, that he had been in church from the beginning of the service to the end of it. He was, therefore, acquitted; while the public were left in the greatest perplexity, to account as they could for this extraordinary discrepancy.

"The young man was well known to the inspectors, and it was in broad daylight that they had met him and placed his name in their books. Neither, it must be remembered, were they seeking for him, nor thinking of him, nor of the woman, about whom there existed neither curiosity nor suspicion. Least of all, would they have sought her where she was, but for the hint given to them.

"The interest excited, at the time, was very great; but no natural explanation of the mystery has ever been suggested."

The Fetch

In Ireland the doppelganger or, as they would term it, "the Fetch," is a well known part of the country folk's traditional supernatural lore where the double of one suffering from a mortal illness and confined to his bed is sometimes seen to stroll in an unhurried manner through a field, often to then unexpectedly vanish. If the Fetch is seen in the morning it believed to foretell good fortune and a long life. If, however, the Fetch is seen at night, it is believed to be a portent of death. If the Fetch appears "agitated or eccentric in its motions, a violent or painful death" can be expected.

While, it is easy to dismiss such a belief as superstitious nonsense, the nineteenth century

British newspaper editor and investigative journalist, William T. Stead, reported a correspondent in the north of England writing to him with the following story:

"The most startling case that I know of is that of a clergyman who was once in charge of a parish in Ireland.

"Late one night he was sent for by a parishioner who was seriously ill. He had to pass from his house through the churchyard to the village. It was a beautiful moonlight night, and his brother, a medical man, who happened to be staying with him at the time, accompanied him to the village, and waited for his return from the sickroom.

"On their way back to the parsonage, a figure glided past them and the churchyard which they both saw distinctly in the moonlight, and after proceeding so far along the path it turned off and disappeared among the gravestones.

"As it was a most unusual incident at that time of night, they went to the place where they thought the disappearance had taken place, but not a trace could they find.

"The next morning they learnt that the sick man had died, and, more singular still, he was buried in the exact spot where the figure had disappeared. It is some time since I was told the story, but you had better write to the clergyman in question."

Mr. Stead wrote to the clergyman inquiring as to whether the incident had actually occurred.

"I cannot imagine where you get your information from," the clergyman responded, "but the facts of the case are as you have stated.

"What I saw, whether ghost or specter, was seen by me in exceedingly bright moonlight, as I returned from visiting a dying man across the churchyard of Fens, County of Wexford, in the year 1849. I was accompanied by one of my brothers, a captain, then staying with me, who also saw and recognized the specter, or phantom, or ghost, or whatever you may be pleased to call it. My own family are well acquainted with the fact.

"All the same, I never said I saw a ghost, but that I did see something I could not at all account for, and which at the time did not affect either of us as a ghost should have done, viz., by the hair of our heads standing up, etc. We were so little affected by what we saw that we followed the appearance in amongst the graves to find out what any person could possibly be doing there at that time; but the strange part of the matter is that two days after I buried the man at the very spot where he disappeared."

The Physician's Fetch

A final, dramatic example of the Fetch was recounted by the noted Irish writer and folklorist, Patrick Kennedy, who wrote, "an unexplained mystery has been communicated to us. It is here given without any further commentary than our assurance of the good faith of our informant, who equally vouched for the veracity of her authorities, one of them being the principal witness of the apparition.

"In one of our Irish cities, and in a room where the mild moonbeams of a summer night were resting on the carpet and on a table near the window, Mrs. B., wife of a doctor in good practice and general esteem, looking towards this window from her pillow, was startled by the appearance of her husband, standing near the table just mentioned, and seeming to look with attention on a book that was lying open on it. Now the living and breathing man was lying by her side, apparently asleep; and greatly as she was surprised and affected, she had sufficient command of herself to remain without movement, lest she should expose him to the terror which she herself at the moment experienced. After gazing at the apparition for a few seconds, she bent her eyes on her husband, to ascertain if his looks were turned in the direction of the window, but his eyes were closed. She turned round again, though dreading the sight of what she now felt certain to be her husband's fetch, but it was no longer there. She lay sleepless throughout the remainder of the night, but still bravely refrained from disturbing her partner.

"Next morning Dr. B. seeing signs of disquiet in his wife's countenance while at breakfast, made some affectionate inquiries, but she concealed her trouble; and at his ordinary hour he sallied forth to make his calls.

"Meeting Dr. C. in the street, and falling into conversation with him, he asked his opinion on the subject of fetches.

"'I think' was the answer, 'and so I am sure do you, that they are mere illusions, produced by a disturbed stomach acting upon the excitable brain of a highly imaginative or superstitious person.'

"'Then,' said Dr. B., 'I am highly imaginative or superstitious, for I distinctly saw my own outward man last night, standing at the table in the bedroom, and clearly distinguishable in the moonlight. I am afraid my wife saw it too, but I have been afraid to speak to her on the subject.'

"'You have acted like a sensible man; but now be off to your patients, as I must run to mine.'

"About the same hour on the ensuing night the poor lady was again roused, but by a more painful circumstance. She felt her husband moving convulsively, and immediately after he cried to her in low and interrupted accents, 'Ellen, dear, I am suffocating. Send for Dr. C.'

"She sprang up, huddled on some clothes, and, without waiting for the slow movements of the servant, she ran to his house. He came with all speed, but his efforts for his friend were useless. He had burst a large blood vessel in the lungs, and was soon beyond human aid.

"In the passionate lamentations which the bereaved wife could not restrain in the presence of the physician, she frequently cried out, 'Oh! The fetch! The fetch!' At a later period she told him of the appearance the night before her husband's death; and he thoroughly believed her statement."

Grave Relics

If someday, by some chance, someone should happen to offer you a human skull, an Egyptian mummy or some other similarly macabre relic of the dead, you might want to think twice before accepting the offer.

The Murderer's Skull

The writer, R. Thurston Hopkins, grew up in Gyves House, the former residence of the governor of Bury Gaol in Bury St. Edmunds, Suffolk, England. His father, F. C. Hopkins, had bought the prison, complete with the cells, high walled exercise yard and gallows. And it was upon the gallows of Bury Gaol, in August of 1828, that the infamous "Red Barn Murderer," William Corder, was executed. Following the execution, according to the lurid customs of the time, Corder's corpse was dissected by the prison surgeon, his scalp pickled, his skin tanned and his skeleton given to the local hospital where it served as an instructional aid for medical students.

When, many years later, the surgeon died, he left the pickled scalp and tanned skin to a local doctor by the name of Kilner who, one day decided it might be nice to add William Corder's skull to his collection of grisly relics.

As Dr. Kilner removed Corder's skull from his skeleton, he felt a most disconcerting "something" which gave him a momentary reason for second thoughts. Still, he was a man who was known to scorn what he referred to as "this mumbo jumbo nonsense about ghosts." He wired another skull to the skeleton, had Corder's skull nicely polished, placed it in a fine ebony box and he displayed his prize in a cabinet in the drawing room of his home.

A few days later, at around seven in the evening, a maid announced that a gentleman wished to see him in the surgery.

"Is he someone you know?" Dr. Kilner enquired.

"No, I have never seen him before," the servant replied, adding that the caller was "a proper old-fashioned" looking gentleman, wearing a "furry top hat and a blue overcoat with silver buttons."

Somewhat irritated at being bothered past normal business hours, Kilner made his way to the surgery, his servant following behind him with a lamp. He felt that someone was waiting in the darkness but, when the maid entered with her lamp, it became clear that the room was empty.

A few evenings later, as the doctor gazed out his drawing room window, he saw a man loitering outside on the lawn — a man wearing a beaver top hat and a greatcoat from an earlier era. As the doctor stepped outside to get a closer look, the gentleman melted away into nothingness.

Soon the tranquility of Kilner's nights was to be perpetually disturbed by the perplexing sounds of doors opening by themselves, footsteps echoing throughout the house, heavy breathing, muttering coming from the other side of bedroom doors, and hammering and crying emanating from the drawing room below. Sleep became almost impossible.

By now, Dr. Kilner had reevaluated his previous dismissive attitude toward what he had once called "this mumbo jumbo nonsense about ghosts" and he was certain that all of his troubles were due to the polished skull in the ebony box in his drawing room.

But what could he do? If he replaced the now highly polished skull onto Corder's skeleton, the difference would surely be noticed.

Then, one night, he was awakened by a loud noise which, it seemed, had come from downstairs. After cowering in bed for several minutes, Kilner lit a candle and silently made his way to the staircase landing. By the candle's light, he could see the faceted glass handle of the drawing room door. An eerie white, dismembered hand appeared and turned the handle, opening the door. Wielding a heavy candlestick as a weapon, Kilner raced down the staircase toward the drawing room. As he reached the open door, a powerful force of wind tore past him, extinguishing his candle. He entered the room, struggling to light a match. The drawing room floor was strewn with thousands of ebony splinters. The door to the cabinet had been thrown open. In the flickering light cast by his match, Dr. Kilner could clearly see the polished skull, which now rested upon a cabinet shelf, seeming to leer at him with what appeared to be an evil grin.

The doctor was now certain that he needed to rid himself of the skull. He begged Hopkins' father to take the skull. "As you are the owner of Corder's condemned cell and the gallows on which he was hanged, perhaps it won't hurt you to take care of his skull," Kilner argued.

As the elder Hopkins made his way back to Gyves House with the skull wrapped in a silk handkerchief, he twisted his foot on a hotel step and fell just as Lady Gage, a local aristocrat, happened to be passing by. The highly polished skull slipped from Hopkins' hands and rolled toward Lady Gage's feet. The lady screamed, gave Hopkins an accusatory look and quickly made her way past him.

Due to his twisted foot, Hopkins' father was confined to his bed for a week. The day after he accepted the skull, his best mare fell into a chalk pit and broke her back. The months which followed brought Hopkins further sorrows. Several previously successful real estate ventures in which he had partnered with Doctor Kilner suffered heavy losses and both men were brought close to bankruptcy.

Attributing all of this to the skull, Hopkins' father took it to a churchyard in the countryside and bribed a gravedigger to bury it in consecrated soil. Upon doing so, his luck changed for the better and the curse of the skull appeared to have been lifted.

The Egyptian Dancer's Foot

Should you still not be convinced of the need to avoid such relics of the dead, you might consider the following events recorded by Jessie Adelaide Middleton in her *White Ghost Book* which I shall relate entirely in her own words:

"Last New Year's Eve, Miss Westwood, a girl friend who was staying with us, went to a New Year's party, after the theatre, at the Moulin d'Or Restaurant in Church Street, Soho. Among the guests was a traveler who had been in the East a great deal and spoke several languages. I will call him Mr. Stanhope, though that is not his real name. Just before the clock struck twelve, he took from his pocket a mummy's foot and held it up, saying, 'Which of you would like to have this for a mascot?' The girls who were there all uttered exclamations of horror and disgust; the men laughed.

"The foot — a woman's — was passed round and examined with awe and shuddering. It was in beautiful condition, every toe and even the nails being perfect, in color dark brown, almost black with age and bitumen, but having scraps of the cerement cloth still clinging to it. The shape was slender, the foot beautifully formed, the size hardly larger than that of a child, though, of course, it was much shrunken. Mr. Stanhope said that, according to the hieroglyphics on the coffin, it had been the foot of an Egyptian dancer.

"When everybody had looked long enough at it, my friend Miss Westwood, who is very practical and matter-of-fact, and does not believe — did not, rather — in occult influence, said, 'Let me have it — just for fun — just to see if it brings me any luck.'

"Mr. Stanhope, with an air of great relief — which they all took to be assumed for a joke — handed it to her.

"'It will bring you luck — eventually,' he said; 'but you may have some bad luck just at first, before it does so. Are you nervous?'

"'No,' she said, 'not a bit; I don't believe in such things.'

"She wrapped the foot up in her lace handkerchief and put it in her bag, and presently the party broke up. I gathered afterwards from her own lips all that had happened.

"Miss Westwood arrived home with the mummy's foot in her bag, and as she was our guest I was sitting up for her. She took it out of her bag and showed it to me at once — much to my horror, for I am by no means in favor of such 'mascots.' To begin with, I think that to carry portions of an embalmed body about, however long ago they may have been entombed, is not only irreverent, but is downright desecration. Also, because I have known queer things about mummies and mummy influence; and the foot, though I examined it at first with great interest, repulsed me terribly.

"'Do take it upstairs, if you must keep it,' I said, 'and never let me see it again while you are in the house.'

"Miss Westwood laughed and joked, and carried off the mummy's foot, which she put in a bookcase in her bedroom, which was on the floor above mine, making a niche for it by moving some of the books.

"The next night, or rather early morning, she woke up suddenly with the feeling that there was some Presence in the room. It was, she described later, as if there was someone quite close to the bed, but she saw absolutely nothing. She sat up in bed, more terrified than she had ever been in her life, and instinctively called out, but not loudly. Her impression was that as she called out there was no longer any cause for alarm, because the Presence was no longer there. The mummy's foot never entered her thoughts; in fact, she had forgotten its very existence, as she was not in the least bit superstitious.

"So strongly did the incident fix itself on her mind that the first words she said to me when she came down to breakfast were, 'I had such a strange experience in the night — it was just as if there was someone in my room. By the by, did you come in while I was asleep for anything, and go out quietly?'

"These words made me feel very uncomfortably for I had had exactly the same experience as she had herself, and related it to her; and then we compared notes and found that it had been at exactly the same hour, which was proved in each case by the church clock striking four. So disturbed was our rest for the fortnight that the mummy's foot remained in the house that we both longed to get rid of it. Not only were we awakened during the night with the eerie feeling that there was Somebody or Something moving about quite close to us, but at all hours of the day there would come stealing over the house the horror of an invisible malign Presence, which terrified us even more than anything more tangible would have done. The impression was like 'darkness that can be felt' we saw nothing, and yet trembled with fear, 'All imagination!' the skeptic will say; but it must be remembered that Miss Westwood, at any rate, was both skeptical and unimaginative, and it was only after several days that she suggested 'it really must be something to do with the mummy's foot.'

"She thereupon decided not to keep it, and disposed of it as quickly as she could. After that we had peace, and a cloud seemed lifted from the house.

"A few months later, Miss Westwood and I were both at a supper party at a friend's house at Hampstead, and met Mr. Stanhope, who also happened to be there, with his wife. After greeting him, Miss Westwood said, 'Well, it was kind of you to give me that mummy's foot; it is perfectly horrid, and has had a dreadful effect on us all.'

"'I told you it might bring you some bad luck before it brought you good,' he said, 'and if you had kept it I think it would have been lucky. But now you have sent it away I may as well tell you that there was something uncanny about it; so much so that I can say candidly that I was delighted when you accepted it that night at the Moulin d'Or.'

"'I stole the foot, as I told you, from an ancient tomb in Egypt, and it really is the foot of a dancer, for her history was told in the colored inscription on the inside of the coffin. I brought it back with me to

England because it was a really beautiful specimen, and I kept it with me because I rather like such things. I was not married then, and was living in rooms at Kensington. My landlady was a dear old soul, friendly and garrulous, and I had often stayed with her before. One evening last winter, when she was bringing up my dinner, she was crying, and in answer to my questions told me that she was very worried about one of her children, whom she was sure was light-headed and must be ill or was going crazy. The child, she said, kept saying she saw a black naked foot peeping in and out from under the curtain of the kitchen dresser downstairs. She could talk of nothing else, and was simply terrified.'

"'Well, that is extraordinary,' I said; 'bring her up here after dinner and let me talk to her.'

"'Yes, I will,' said my landlady.'

"'After she had left the room I unwrapped the mummy's foot and placed it on the mantelpiece in full view. Hitherto I had kept it locked away in a box out of sight.'

"'The landlady presently brought up the child, a pretty little girl of about three or four years old. I did not mention what her mother had told me, but talked to her about dolls and kittens and various other things children like. As we were chatting she looked with childish curiosity about my room, and suddenly, as her eyes fell on the mantelpiece, she screamed out

— 'Mother! Mother! There's the foot! — There's the foot!' and began howling and screaming as if she saw a ghost.'

"'After that I felt it was time to part with it, for it was something more than a bit of a white elephant; for the child stuck to her guns, and described exactly how the foot used to appear and disappear under the curtain that hung round the lower part of the kitchen dresser, as if it was dancing. The way she told it — in simple, childish words — was sufficiently convincing, one could not but believe her; and she could never have heard of the foot at all, for I had kept it carefully locked up.'

"'When I met you at the Moulin d'Or I was wondering what I should do with it. By a sudden inspiration I made up my mind to offer it round as a mascot. Perhaps it was not a very considerate thing to do, after the child's story, but these things do affect different people in different ways, and you might have experienced nothing at all. What did you experience, by the way? I am most curious to hear.'

"When we told him, he said he was glad for our sakes we had parted with it. 'All the same,' he added, 'I wish I had left the thing safe in its coffin, instead of letting it go loose in the world. These things can be very devilish. It will be a lesson to me next time.'"

The Phantom House

Is it possible that certain places offer a portal into the past where one might observe centuries old events replaying themselves out again and again complete with long ago demolished physical landmarks? If so, Knighton Gorges on the Isle of Wight may be one such place.

Undoubtedly one of the most beautiful houses on the Isle of Wight was the ivy covered, grey stone gothic styled manor house near the village of Newchurch known as Knighton Gorges. With parts of the house dating back to the eleventh century Knighton Gorges played a highly important role in island's history.

The name Knighton comes from the Celtic word "Keithan," which means "the place of a fight," a name highly appropriate for an estate whose owners, throughout its history, were often engaged in bloody conflicts. As early as the fourteenth century, ghostly moans and wailing were said to emanate from the room in which Sir Theobald Russell died from wounds sustained while defending the island from French invaders.

When, in the sixteenth century, a new owner remodeled parts of the manor, in the course of adding new additions to the house, screams and the rattling of chains filled the air while the furnishings of the haunted room flew about with such frequency that it became necessary to call for a priest to conduct a, perhaps, not altogether successful exorcism.

In the eighteenth century, Knighton Gores became both the scene of a suicide and the focus of a notorious scandal. Finally, in the early nineteenth century, the then owner had the great manor house demolished in order to both eliminate its costly maintenance and to lessen his tax load. But that would not be the last Knighton Gorges.

Many years later, a young traveler sought shelter at a house in Newchurch on a cold winter's night. Over a much appreciated dinner, he complained to his hosts of how earlier that evening he had been almost run down by a carriage pulled by two horses racing up a drive leading to a grand house. Rightly upset by this, he had made his way to the house seeking recompense for this indignity.

Once there, he heard music coming from inside the house but no one heeded his insistent knocking on the door. He peered into a window and, through a small opening between the curtains, he could see what appeared to be a costume party taking place in the drawing room with all of the guests attired in Georgian dress. He began rapping on the window but, as nothing he did succeeded in gaining the partygoers' attention, he finally gave up and made his way to Newchurch.

The young man's story seemed impossible to his hosts as they were unaware of any such house existing anywhere in the vicinity. When their guest showed them the house's location on a map, they were stunned, for he had pointed to the exact site of the long ago demolished Knighton Gorges.

Over the years others reported the occasional reappearance of the phantom manor as well as hearing music emanating from the house site. It was not, however, until the 1916 publication of some rather extraordinary experiences which had occurred only a few years earlier that outsiders became aware of the strange phenomena which so often occurred on the grounds of the Knighton Gorges estate.

Miss Ethel C. Hargrove, a Fellow of the Royal Geographical Society, reported that in 1913, on a cold New Year's Eve, she, her sister and three local villagers had walked a mile from Newchurch to the grounds of the former Knighton Gorges Manor a little before midnight and they were rewarded for their having braved the cold when, at ten minutes to twelve, they experienced what she described as the "marvelous aural manifestation of a lady singing soprano." This was followed by a duet with a baritone and part songs accompanied by a spinet or harpsichord.

"Lastly came some very dainty and refined minuet airs. A few minutes before midnight, a flood of melody arose from the site of the former mansion. It was varied in character — dance music played on a harpsichord, Georgian minuet airs, slow and stately, then, a duet between tenor and soprano voices. At twelve, the party seemed to break up, a pistol or gun was fired, dogs bayed, and the sound of carriage wheels was heard."

"One summer evening, later that year," her account continues, "I was walking on the road that passes the old gateposts, between the hours of seven and eight, earnestly engrossed in conversation with a friend. My attention was suddenly arrested by a very loud noise, apparently made by children playing with wire railings. We could not ascertain the cause, but as there were several schoolboys about, we passed on and thought no more of the circumstance.

"It never would have occurred to me to give the matter another thought but for this coincidence. A few days later, on Monday 6th July, I was sitting on the fallen trunks shortly before 8 p.m. The thought of hearing again the mysterious music was strong within me, but I was destined to hear music of a different kind.

"Again, it delighted my ears, but this time it was the voices of a church choir. I listened with great joy till I was disturbed by conflicting elements — the self-same noise I had attributed to the schoolboys knocking the wire railings.

"This time it was simply deafening. 'Children playing again,' I reasoned, but it had in it an affinity to the clashing of swords. 'Do be quiet,' I shouted, for the sacred music was hardly distinguishable in such a din. Finding my remonstrance had no effect, I rose to my feet and approached the spot from whence the tumult proceeded — the corner of the walled garden. When I arrived there, it ceased, but neither boys nor railings could be seen.

"Surely in days of yore," she concluded, "a mortal conflict must have taken place there, and even now the forces of good and evil appear to war against each other."

"Two years later on New Year's Eve, 1915, I determined to revisit Knighton with a friend who had never been there before. We walked from Newchurch with a view of arriving in good time for any manifestations. While walking, I heard the sounds of distant music intermingled with the bleating of the sheep, but I did not at the time make any remark on the subject.

"The night was fine and starlit, and the wind played gently through the bare branches of the trees. There were no lights in the cottages and, even at 9 p.m., the world seemed asleep. As we approached Knighton, lights were reflected from behind our shoulders, so vivid that we could plainly see our own shadows in dark relief, and I had the sensation that people were following us, but whenever I looked behind the dim gloom was unbroken except for the twinkling of the stars, and there was not a soul in sight.

"We settled ourselves at the old gates to await the trend of events, but a vague feeling of discomfort that I was sitting in someone's way, obsessed me, so we decided to move to another gate across the road leading into a broad expanse of field, merging into the long range of downs.

"The field was studded with lights, apparently reflected from the windows of a house, and my friend had a strong impression that we were there just in time to witness the advent of some late arrivals; she could hear the deep baying of house dogs and the shriller yap of a King Charles or a Blenheim spaniel.

"As the door opened to admit the guests, my friend plainly saw a square white house with ivy covering the lower part, leaded diamond panes to the windows, and heard all the sounds of welcoming and greeting — a confused murmur of voices. Next, a flute and violin could be distinctly heard. Then came silence; and a man's form could be plainly seen standing near a bow window with a tall-stemmed glass with a flat bowl, raised as if for a toast.

"He was dressed in eighteenth-century costume; black clothes, frilled shirt, white silk stockings; his dark hair plainly tied back with a black ribbon. There was evidently cheering and clapping of hands; then a burst of music, and this time the drum could be plainly distinguished.

"From then until 11:40 p.m. there were no sounds except an occasional burst of music, and fainter moving lights spread over a large area. And reflected on the opposite side of the road, one could plainly see the posts and even the twigs of the bare hawthorns in the hedges.

"I walked up and down the road a little way, to keep warm, and, when I rejoined my friend, twice I turned towards the wrong opening, misled by the powerful light. At twenty to twelve, when we were standing in the road opposite the phantom house, a full tenor voice lustily gave forth 'God rest you, merry gentlemen,' and the whole party joined in the chorus.

"The lights of the house were soon so dim that one could see nothing, though curiously enough, the reflections on the far side remained as vivid. We heard nothing more except two weird sounds, which my friend thought the hoot of a motor. I took them to be the call for a belated carriage.

"Evidently the revels were at an end, and we lost no time in taking our departure, for we had a lonely walk of five miles across country to Sandown. It was worth it, we declared, although we did not reach our destination until after 2 a.m."

In the years since a number of people have seen the phantom house, heard ghostly music, seen or heard the sound of a horse drawn carriage thundering down the drive and have seen such ghostly figures near the Knighton Gorges gateposts as a lady in an ornate mauve ball gown, children without faces in dirty pinafores, a faceless woman in a long white hooded garment, a grey man in old-fashioned clothes and a man wearing a cape and top hat. As a result, a highly popular annual tradition has developed of ghost enthusiasts gathering at the gateposts on New Year's Eve in the hope of experiencing the phenomena themselves.

Stranger still, motorists stopping by the gateposts or merely driving by have often experienced the total loss of their car's electrical power or their engine failing completely. In the days before cell phones the owners of a nearby farm house had so many motorists knocking on their door asking to use their phone to call for a tow truck that they had a pay phone installed on their porch!

And, then, there is the mystery of the gatepost lions. For decades Ted Perry, a tour bus driver, had stopped at the gateposts to tell his passengers the history of Knighton Gorges and, for decades, he had stated that the gateposts topped with heraldic lions were, now, all that remained of the once grand estate. Then, one day in 1972, upon making his regular stop at the gateposts, he was stunned to see that the stone lions were no longer there. Concerned that they might have been stolen, he fired off a letter to the local newspaper asking if anyone knew what had become of them.

When it was pointed out to him that there had never been stones lions or anything similar to lions atop the pillars, a controversy ensued which was to rage for years. Although the earliest known photograph of the pillars, published in 1916, clearly shows the pillars without lions or a stone animal of any kind, numerous locals flocked to Perry's defense reporting that they, also, had in recent times seen lions or griffins or some such stone carvings atop the pillars. In one case a woman testified to clearly seeing a stone lion atop one of the pillars, only to then see it begin to shimmer and vanish. Another local reported having seen the stone lions when visiting the site at night but never during daylight hours.

Gay Baldwin, a historian who conducts ghost tours on the Isle of Wight and who has written eight books on the subject, decided to investigate and discovered that at one time in the distant past the gateposts were called the "dog pillars" because well over a century ago there had been stone dogs perched atop the pillars but, she was told, an earlier owner of the property had taken them away to decorate another of his estates.

Gay later compared the remaining part of the pillar tops with a diamond shape board hanging in the local church displaying the coat of arms of a member of one of the families which had once owned Knighton Gorges. She found that the remaining parts of the stone carvings atop the pillars match exactly the wreath and coronet worn upon the helmet surmounting the family's coat of arms. And rising above the coronet was the family crest: a dog. That being the case, it seems clear that what remains today atop the pillars is only the lower half of a family crest, a crest which, at one time, would have been topped by the sculpture of a dog, a sculpture which could, from a distance, easily be mistaken for a heraldic lion.

And so the mystery of Knighton Gorges continues. Is Knighton Gorges a place in which both the present and the past exist simultaneously?

Are there supernatural forces at work which science cannot, yet, explain? I have no answers. I know only that the extraordinary events which I have recounted within these pages are absolutely true.

The Versailles Adventure

Another place where it might be possible to walk into the past, where one might observe physical landmarks which no longer exist, encounter individuals long since dead and, perhaps, even interact with them is the parkland adjacent to the Petit Trianon on the grounds of the Palace of Versailles.

On the 10th of August, 1901, while visiting the Palace of Versailles, two English schoolteachers of impeccable character and credentials, Miss Charlotte Anne Moberly, the Principal of St. Hugh's College at Oxford and Eleanor Jourdain, her Vice-Principal, entered into one of the most intriguing and controversial adventures ever recorded within the annals of parapsychological investigation.

After spending some time touring the Palace, the ladies decided to next visit the Petite Trianon, a smaller palace situated at the other end of the royal estate grounds. Although they had a map, they soon became lost.

"We walked for some distance down a wooded alley," Miss Jourdain later wrote, "and then came upon the buildings of the Grand Trianon. We went on in the direction of the Petit Trianon, but just before reaching what we knew afterwards to be the main entrance I saw a gate leading to a path cut deep below the level of the ground above, and as the way was open and had the look of an entrance that was used, I said, 'Shall we try this path? It must lead to the house,' and we followed it.

"To our right we saw some farm-buildings looking empty and deserted; farm implements (among others a plough) were lying about; we looked in, but saw no one. The impression was saddening, but it was not until we reached the crest of the rising ground where there was a garden that I began to feel as if we had lost our way, and as if something were wrong. There were two men there in official dress (greenish in color), with something in their hands; it might have been a staff. A wheelbarrow and some other gardening tools were near them. They told us, in answer to my enquiry, to go straight on. I remember repeating my question, because they answered in a seemingly casual and mechanical way, but only got the same answer in the same manner.

"As we were standing there I saw to the right of us a detached solidly-built cottage, with stone steps at the door. A woman and a girl were standing at the doorway, and I particularly noticed their unusual dress; both wore white kerchiefs tucked into the bodice, and the girl's dress, though she looked thirteen or fourteen only, was down to her ankles. The woman was passing a jug to the girl who wore a close white cap.

"Following the directions of the two men we walked on but the path pointed out to us seemed to lead away from where we imagined the Petit Trianon to be and there was a feeling of depression and loneliness about the place. I began to feel as if I were walking in my sleep; the heavy dreaminess was oppressive.

"At last we came upon a path crossing ours, and saw in front of us a building consisting of some columns roofed in, and set back in the trees. Seated on the steps was a man with a heavy black cloak round his shoulders, and wearing a slouch hat. At that moment the eerie feeling which had begun in the garden culminated in a definite impression of something uncanny and fear-inspiring.

"The man slowly turned his face, which was marked by smallpox; his complexion was very dark. The expression was very evil and yet unseeing, and though I did not feel that he was looking particularly at us, I felt a repugnance to going past him. But I did not wish to show the feeling, which I thought was meaningless, and we talked about the best way to turn, and decided to go to the right.

"Suddenly we heard a man running behind us: he shouted, 'Mesdames, Mesdames,' and when I turned he said in an accent that seemed to me unusual that our way lay in another direction. 'Il ne faut pas passer par la.' ('You shouldn't go there.') He then made a gesture, adding 'par ici cherchez la maison.' ('Over there look for the house.') Though we were surprised to be addressed, we were glad of the direction, and I thanked him. The man ran off with a curious smile on his face: the running ceased as abruptly as it had begun, not far from where we stood. I remember that the man was young-looking, with a florid complexion and rather long dark hair. I do not remember the dress, except that the material was dark and heavy, and that the man wore buckled shoes.

"We walked on, crossing a small bridge that went across a green bank, high on our right hand and shelving down below as to a very small overshadowed pool of water glimmering some way off. A tiny stream descended from above us, so small as to seem to lose itself before reaching the little pool. We then followed a narrow path till almost immediately we came upon the English garden front of the Petit Trianon.

"The place was deserted but as we approached the terrace I remember drawing my skirt away with a feeling as though someone were near and I had to make room, and then wondering why I did it. While we were on the terrace a boy came out of the door of a second building which opened on it, and I still have the sound in my ears of his slamming it behind him. He directed us to go round to the other entrance, and seeing us hesitate, with the peculiar smile of suppressed mockery, offered to show us the way.

"We passed through the French garden, part of which was walled in by trees. The feeling of dreariness was very strong there, and continued till we actually reached the front entrance to the Petit Trianon."

The impression of dreariness returned to Miss Jourdain from time to time but the two women did not speak of their strange experience until when, at least a week later, Miss Moberly asked, "Do you think the Petit Trianon is haunted?"

Miss Jourdain quickly answered, "Yes, I do."

They did not speak of their experience again until three months later when Miss Moberly "casually mentioned" having seen a woman sitting on a seat on the lawn by the terrace of the Petit Trianon. Upon doing so, she was stunned to discover that the woman had not been seen by Miss Jourdain.

"The lady," Miss Moberly later wrote, "was sitting, holding out a paper as though to look at it at arm's length. I supposed her to be sketching. It seemed as though she must be making a study of trees, for they grew close in front of her, and there seemed to be nothing else to sketch.

"She saw us and, when we passed close by on her left hand, she turned and looked full at us.

"It was not a young face, and (though rather pretty) it did not attract me. She had on a shady white (straw) hat, perched on a good deal of fair hair that fluffed round her forehead. Her light summer dress was arranged on her shoulders in handkerchief fashion, and there was a little line of either green or gold near the edge of the handkerchief, which showed me that it was over, not tucked into, her bodice, which was cut low. Her dress was longwaisted, with a good deal of fullness in the skirt, which seemed to be short. There was something unattractive about her expression, and after looking full at her, I suddenly turned away."

The two ladies began to compare their individual recollections of the day and Miss Jourdain was surprised to learn that Miss Moberly had not seen the cottage with the woman passing a jug to the girl she remembered so clearly seeing while Miss Moberly had seen two women Miss Jourdain had not seen; both the woman who appeared to be sketching and a woman shaking a white cloth from the window of another building. Miss Moberly had also been struck by a feeling of "extraordinary depression" during the visit and a sense that there was an unnatural, flat, two dimensional look to the landscape "as though painted on canvas" or "worked in tapestry." Intrigued, the ladies decided to independently write accounts of their experience and to learn everything they could about the area around the Petit Trianon.

Searching for an explanation Miss Moberly learned that the 10th of August, the day of their visit to Versailles, was the anniversary of the sacking of the Tuileries, the day the palace in Paris fell to the French Revolution. Three days later, King Louis XVI and Marie Antoinette were arrested.

Miss Moberly also was told by a friend living in Paris that "she remembered hearing from friends at Versailles that on a certain day in August Marie Antoinette is regularly seen sitting outside the garden front at the Petit Trianon, with a light flapping hat and a pink dress." Moreover the entire area around the Petite Trianon, the garden, the path by the water and especially the Hamlet (a small, fully staffed village built for Marie Antoinette in which she and her court amused themselves by pretending to be country peasants) "are peopled with those who used to be with her there; in fact that all the occupations and amusements reproduce themselves there for a day and a night."

On January 2nd, 1902, a cold and wet day, Miss Jourdain visited Versailles for a second time. She did not, at first, experience the eerie sensation she had felt during her visit in August. "But," she later wrote, "on crossing a bridge to go to the Hamlet, the old feeling returned in full force; it was as if I had crossed a line and was suddenly in a circle of influence. To the left I saw a tract of park-like ground, the trees bare and very scanty.

"I noticed a cart being filled with sticks by two laborers, and thought I could go to them for directions if I lost my way. The men wore tunics and capes with pointed hoods of bright colors, a sort of terra-cotta red and the other deep blue. I turned aside for an instant — not more — to look at the Hamlet, and when I looked back the men and cart were completely out of sight, and this surprised me, as I could see a long way in every direction. And though I had seen the men in the act of loading the cart with sticks, I could not see any trace of them on the ground either at the time or afterwards.

"I did not, however, dwell upon any part of the incident, but went on to the Hamlet. The houses were all built near a sheet of water, and the old oppressive feeling of the last year was noticeable, especially under the balcony of the Maison de la Reine (Queen's House,) and near a window in what I afterwards found to be the Laiterie (Dairy.) I really felt a great reluctance to go near the window or look in, and when I did so I found it shuttered inside.

"Coming away from the Hamlet I at last reached a building, which I knew to be the smaller Orangerie. I turned back by mistake into the park and found myself in a wood, so thick that though I had turned towards the Hamlet I could not see it. Before I entered I looked across an open space towards a belt of trees to the left of the Hamlet some way off, and noticed a man, cloaked like those we had seen before, slip swiftly through the line of trees. The smoothness of his movement attracted my attention.

"I was puzzling my way among the maze of paths in the wood when I heard a rustling behind me which made me wonder why people in silk dresses came out on such a wet day; and I said to myself, 'just like French people.' I turned sharply round to see who they were, but saw no one, and then, all in a moment, I had the same feeling as by the terrace in the summer, only in a much greater degree; it was as though I were closed in by a group of people who already filled the path, coming from behind and passing me. At one moment there seemed really no room for me. I heard some women's voices talking French, and caught the words 'Monsieur and Madame' said close to my ear. The crowd got scarce and drifted away, and then faint music as of a band, not far off, was audible. It was playing very light music with a good deal of repetition in it. Both voices and music were diminished in tone, as in a phonograph, unnaturally. The pitch of the band was lower than usual. The sounds were intermittent, and once more I felt the swish of a dress close by me.

"I looked at the map which I had with me, but whenever I settled which path to take I felt impelled to go by another. After turning backwards and forwards many times I at last found myself back at the Orangerie, and was overtaken by a gardener. He had hair on his face, a grizzled beard, was large and loosely made. His height was very uncommon, and he seemed to be of immense strength. His arms were long and very muscular. I noticed that even through the sleeves of his jersey. I asked him where I should find the Queen's grotto. He told me to follow the path I was on, and, in answer to a question, said that I must pass the Belvedere, adding that it was quite impossible to find one's way about the park unless one had been brought up in the place, and so used to it that 'personne ne pourrait vous tromper.' ('No one can deceive you.') The expression specially impressed me because of the experience I had just had in the wood. He pointed out the way and left me. The path led past the Belvedere, which I took for granted was the building we had seen in August, for coming upon it from behind, all the water was hidden from me. I made my way from there to the French garden without noticing the paths I took.

"On my return to Versailles I made careful enquiries as to whether the band had been playing there that day, but was told that though it was the usual day of the week, it had not played because it had played the day before, being New Year's Day.

"I told my French friends of my walk, and they said that there was a tradition of Marie Antoinette having been seen making butter within the Dairy and for that reason it was shuttered."

Over the next few years, the two ladies continued to research the history of the area in the vicinity of the Trianons and the Hamlet in the hope of understanding what they had encountered. The obvious answer, that they had seen actors or park attendants in period dress was quickly ruled out. No park employees were dressed in the manner they had seen and official records showed that no motion picture companies or theatrical productions had been given permission to work in the park on the days in question.

But, perhaps, most intriguing of all, many of the physical landmarks they had seen; the woods, the bridge, the ravine, the waterfall and the kiosk, did not exist in the Versailles of 1901.

Could it be, they wondered, that they had not seen ghosts but had actually, somehow, walked into the past?

In 1911 they published a slim volume entitled, *An Adventure*, an account of their experiences in Versailles along with the research which they felt proved the authenticity of all they had seen.

Through researching old maps they found that everything they had seen — but which they had been told had never existed — had, in fact, existed during the time of Marie Antoinette in the exact positions in which they had described them — everything that is except for the small ravine they had crossed by mean of a small bridge.

However, in 1912, they learned that an original map of the Trianon grounds drawn by Richard Mique, the Royal Architect, had been recently discovered in the chimney of an old house. The map clearly showed a small ravine in exactly the same place as they had described it, years before, in *An Adventure*.

As time went on, the ladies were contacted by others who had had similar experiences at Versailles. One of the most intriguing, perhaps, was that of the Crooke family who lived in an apartment overlooking the Versailles grounds during the years 1907 and 1908. Although they could see from their apartment crowds of tourists arriving at the Palace each morning, they rarely saw anyone walking about inside the grounds. In 1908 they began to see people attired in eighteenth century clothing in the area near the Hamlet. Mr. Crooke encountered a man wearing a small three-cornered hat and both he and his wife came upon a woman "in old-fashioned dress picking up sticks." Mr. Crooke also reported hearing phantom music and seeing the cottage which had been seen earlier by Miss Jourdain "with people in old fashioned clothes looking out the window." On two occasions he, his wife and his son all saw the sketching lady who had been described by Miss Moberly. "On both occasions she was dressed in a light cream-colored skirt, white fichu, and white untrimmed flapping hat. The skirt was full and ungathered, and the lady spread it round her. Both times she appeared to be sketching, holding out a paper at some distance, as though judging of it."

In 1974, I visited Versailles, spending almost all of the days of August 9th, 10th and 11th in the area of the Hamlet hoping to experience something along the lines of that which had been experienced by Miss Moberly and Miss Jourdain. Although I did not experience anything out of the ordinary, I was told by a member of the staff at an official visitors' information center that often visitors unaware of the haunting would stop by with tales of their having seen the ghosts of people dressed in clothing of the late 1700's.

On the 10th of August I encountered a European ghost aficionado with whom I attempted to retrace the route followed by the ladies seventy-three years before and together we explored the Hamlet where he felt the dairy to be particularly haunted. While the dairy windows were no longer shuttered, they had been fitted with leaded cobalt blue glass panes which were so dark that I could not seen anything within the building, leading me to believe that a ghostly woman had, indeed, been seen so often within it that the cobalt glass had been installed in order to prevent future sightings.

As the sun began to set that day, we found ourselves caught in a sudden rainstorm and he, my traveling companion and I fled for shelter into Marie Antoinette's Grotto. As we waited for the rain to subside, from within the Grotto we distinctly heard footsteps above us. The European gentleman quickly ran out of the grotto but saw no one there. By the time the rain had stopped the gates to the park had closed and the place was dark and deserted. We found our way to the park gate where, with great embarrassment, we explained our predicament and we were escorted out by a Versailles official.

The initial publication of *An Adventure* created a great deal of public interest and set off a controversy which has yet to be settled. Negative criticisms of *An Adventure* were quickly published. Most of these criticisms were, to my mind, overly simplistic in their assumptions and cavalier in their attitude, accusing the highly intelligent and accomplished Moberly and Jourdain of having bad memories, overactive imaginations and of having done poor research.

In the years which followed, other credible witnesses have come forward who, having no previous knowledge of the haunting, had also encountered individuals in the vicinity of the Hamlet and the Trianons dressed in eighteenth century attire.

Over the decades much ink has continued to be spilt in an attempt to explain away both the experience and the research presented in *An Adventure*. Although much of the criticism was made by serious and objective commentators, I cannot help but think that some of the early, more hostile criticism had its origin in a prejudice against and a resentment toward two women who had achieved prominence in the academic world during a time in which such achievement was thought by most to be the sole domain of men.

The Vanishing Hitchhiker

Can the desire to return to the warmth and security of home at the moment of a crisis persist long past death and result in a ghost which ceaselessly attempts to find its way home?

A San Francisco Legend

The rain poured relentlessly, obscuring their vision and making driving hazardous as Sam Kerns and his companion carefully drove down San Francisco's Mission Street returning home from a party late one night. As they approached First Street, Kerns gradually perceived the faint form of a young woman standing alone on the corner as if waiting for someone. Drawing closer, they were surprised to find that she was dressed only in a thin white evening gown and had neither a coat nor umbrella. Yet she seemed oblivious to the weather. Thinking she might be in trouble, Kerns pulled up to the curb and asked if they might give her a ride home.

"Yes, thank you very much," she answered and the men quickly helped her into the back seat of their coupe. As she was obviously cold and wet, Kerns wrapped a car blanket around her. She volunteered an address near Twin Peaks where she said she lived with her mother but offered no explanation as to how she had become stranded. And, although she answered politely when spoken to, it was clear that her mind was on something else and she remained, otherwise, strangely silent.

As they passed Fifth Street, Kern's companion turned around for a moment to make certain she was alright. To his horror, the back seat was empty! Thinking she might have fainted, he quickly leaned over the seat only to find the damp and discarded blanket lying on the floor.

Immediately, he told Kerns to pull over and they attempted to sort out an explanation. They had both seen and spoken with the woman and, yet, she had disappeared without a trace. They had not made any stops and, even if they had, as their car had only two doors, it would have been impossible for her to have left the car without their having known it.

There was only one way to discover an answer and they began searching out the address given by their mysterious passenger.

They soon found the place and, despite the late hour, a pale light shown from within the sadly neglected house. Hesitantly, they knocked on the front door. It was some time before the sounds of footsteps were heard from within. The two men waited expectantly, wondering what they would say.

At last the door opened to reveal a frail, elderly woman huddled beneath a shawl. Kerns felt uncomfortable as he started to explain the reason for their visit but the old woman seemed to understand and sympathetically placed her hand upon his.

"Yes, I know," she gently interrupted. "You needn't continue. It has happened before. That was my daughter. She was killed in an automobile accident two years ago at the corner of First and Mission. She has often tried to return home."

Legend or Reality?

If this story sounds familiar, there is a very good reason for its familiarity. Similar accounts of vanishing hitchhikers have been told for centuries throughout the world. The phantom hitchhiker has been encountered by solitary walkers, conveyed on horseback, ridden in farm wagons and carriages and has been driven in all manner of automobiles. Although she is most often a woman dressed in party or evening clothes, the hitchhiker, in many instance, is a man. The vanishing hitchhiker is usually encountered at either the site of her death or at the gates of the cemetery in which she was buried. And, sometimes, the story becomes darker when, on a cold or rainy night, the driver offers the lady his coat or sweater. The garment disappears along with the hitchhiker, only to be found later carefully draped over her tombstone.

As a result, tales of the ghostly hitchhiker are often dismissed as being nothing more than legends, said to have happened to a friend of a friend, transplanted from place to place and given the ring of authenticity through the insertion of local place names.

But while this may, indeed, often be the case, is it not possible that the proliferation of similar tales might be the result of the simple fact that the desire to return home at the moment of a fatal accident or other such crises could be so strong and so universal that it could produce ghosts who have behaved in a similar fashion throughout the ages and in every culture? Is it not possible that the plethora of vanishing hitchhiker tales have been the result, not of the mere repetition of an age-old legend, but, instead, of what might rationally be expected from the repetition of such crises throughout time and in every imaginable place coupled with the natural human desire to escape from the trauma of such experiences to a place of safety?

The evidence would suggest that this might well be the case. While, in most instances it proves impossible to track down the identity of those who have actually encountered the vanishing hitchhiker, on occasion, credible witnesses have been identified; witnesses who have recorded their experience for posterity.

No less august a personage than John McLaren, the man who developed San Francisco's Golden Gate Park and served as its Superintendent for fifty-three years, along with others, reported encountering a melancholy young woman dressed in purple standing at dusk by the main park drive near Marx Meadow waiting to be offered a ride home, only to vanish as night falls or upon her reaching the park entrance.

And then there are the numerous more recent and verifiable encounters collected by researchers in England.

The Ghost Leaves a Message

There is the case of the British guitarist and vocalist, Richard Studholme, who, while driving through an area in Kent known as Blue Bell Hill, stopped to give a ride to a girl who asked to be taken to West Kingsdown. After putting her suitcase into the car, off they went. Although she was far from talkative, she asked Mr. Studholme if he might give a message to her parents who resided not far from London in the town of Swanley. After dropping her off in West Kingsdown, the musician called upon her parents as requested, only to learn from the grieving parents that their daughter had been killed two years earlier at the very place at which he had encountered her standing by the roadside. When the paranormal researcher, Michael Goss, interviewed a close friend of the guitarist, he was told, "he's not the sort of person to make up something like that."

The Peddar's Lane Ghost

And there is the experience reported at the time to the Dunstable, Bedfordshire police and printed in the *Dunstable Gazette* of Roy Fulton, a young man, who one evening after a darts match in Leighton Buzzard, was driving through the nearby village of Stanbridge. On a road called Peddar's Lane, he saw a man wearing a white shirt, a dark colored sweater and dark trousers holding out his thumb, gesturing for a ride. Mr. Fulton pulled off to the side of the road. The hitchhiker, whose face seemed strangely pale, opened the car door for himself and sat down beside him. When Mr. Fulton asked where the man was going, the passenger merely pointed in the direction of the road, not saying a single word. When a few minutes later the driver turned to offer the man a cigarette, as he later put it, "The bloke had disappeared."

"I braked, had a quick look in the back to see if he was there. He wasn't and I just gripped the wheel and drove like hell."

This account was backed up by a woman who observed Roy Fulton's agitation following the event. "I was in the Glider that evening," she explained. "I remember Roy coming in. Totally and very visibly shaken...and shaking! More than just a story. This was a real event."

The Ghost with a Flashlight

But, perhaps, most intriguing of all is a ten mile portion of road on the A38 in the area of the market town of Wellington in Somerset which has long been known to be haunted at night by a middle-aged man wearing a long grey overcoat or mackintosh who stands in the middle of the roadway, flashlight in hand, attempting to gain the attention of passing motorists, a haunting which gained notoriety when new sightings were carefully reported in 1970 by the *Western Morning News*.

According to the article in the *Morning News*, a Mrs. K. Swithenbank was driving the A38 towards Taunton when, while rounding a bend, the man appeared without warning in the middle of the road near the Heatherton Grange Hotel. Unable to apply her breaks in time, she immediately swerved her car and almost ended up in a ditch. She was relieved to neither feel nor observe anything suggesting that the man had been hit and, after breaking, she got out of her car intending to admonish the man for being as foolish as to stand in the middle of the road. Amazingly, the man seemed to have vanished. She carefully scanned the area. There was no one to be seen either behind, alongside or in front of her.

Two other motorists reported having exactly the same experience in exactly the same place. Another motorist reported seeing the man in the mackintosh four miles down the road at the village of White Ball.

A motorcyclist, riding through White Ball, however, was not as fortunate as the others. Having swerved to avoid the man in the mackintosh, the rider was thrown from his motorcycle and sustained a broken limb.

On another occasion the phantom was seen by four members of a pop music group at the same time. "We had an engagement up Nottingham way and were driving home," one of the witnesses told the *Morning News*, "the two men in the front and the two girls in the back. We'd heard the story of the ghost being seen only a week or two before and as we approached the stretch of road where it was seen we were talking about it and saying we were getting close to the spot."

"All of a sudden the driver said, 'Look — there it is!' We all saw it, all four of us — a man standing right in the road and looking toward us with an arm outstretched. I said, "Don't stop — drive on fast!' We must have driven right through him."

The reports of all of these incidents compelled Harold Unsworth, a long-haul truck driver from the city of Exeter to relate in a letter to the *Exeter Express and Echo* a series of encounters which he had, quite reasonably, kept secret for twelve years.

He had been driving the A38 when, around three in the morning, about a mile west of Hatherton Grange, he observed a hatless man with long, curly grey hair, wearing a grey or cream colored mackintosh and carrying a flashlight standing out in the pouring rain. Seeing that the man was soaking wet and feeling sorry for him, Mr. Unsworth stopped and offered the man a ride.

The man asked to be driven about four miles down the road to the Beam Bridge at Holcombe. Although the man's speech suggested a good education, Mr. Unsworth was more than a bit unnerved by his guest's desire to recount a series of gruesome accidents which had occurred near the bridge during a one week period of time, giving, with what seemed to be ghoulish enthusiasm, all of the gory details

A few nights later, around 3 a.m., Mr. Unsworth again saw the same man dressed in exactly the same manner standing in the same place he had encountered him before, again standing in the rain, flashlight in hand. Again, Mr. Unsworth offered the man a ride and, again, the man in the mackintosh asked to be let off at the old bridge and, again, his conversation consisted of a recitation of horrific accidents near the old bridge.

Late one night a month later, again around 3 a.m., Mr. Unsworth came upon the man, dressed as before, standing in the rain, his flashlight at the ready. Again, he asked to be dropped off at the bridge and, again, the man's conversation concerned all the unpleasant details of fatal accidents which had taken place in the vicinity of the bridge.

Much to his great relief, Mr. Unsworth was not to encounter the man on his nightly runs for several months.

Then, one night in November of 1958, he, again, saw the man standing in his accustomed place by the A38. Once more, he dropped the man off at the bridge but, on this occasion, his strange passenger asked if Mr. Unsworth might wait for him to pick up what he referred to as "cases" and, then, take him further down the A38 to another place where he wished to be dropped off.

Mr. Unsworth agreed to do so but, when, after waiting twenty minutes, the man had failed to return to his truck, Unsworth decided to continue on without him.

Then, some three miles or so down the road, by Morgan's transport cafe, he saw a figure in his headlights waving a flashlight. "I thought it was a motorist in trouble," Mr. Unsworth explained, "but to my astonishment it was this man. He was shaking his fist at me.

"No other vehicles had passed by to give him a lift to that point. I tried to drive past him, hardy daring to look, but he leapt right in front of my lorry. I braked hard, jack-knifed slightly and stopped. I jumped out and ran back to see what had happened. He stood still in the road again, shaking his fist and cursing me for not having waited for him. He then just turned his back and instantly vanished. My hair stood on end and I ran back to the lorry and drove off as fast as I could!"

Elemental Spirits

I debated a great deal as to whether I should include a discussion of elementals, what some might call "nature spirits," in this book as the evidence for the existence of these entities is far less compelling than is the evidence for ghosts. However, throughout history there have been disconcerting, allegedly true, accounts which give me cause to seriously ponder the possibility of their existence. And, as it is possible that anyone who decides to investigate hauntings might, possibly, encounter these rare and far less understood entities, I decided that it would be highly irresponsible of me if I were not to warn anyone considering explorations into of the realm of the supernatural of the possible dangers they might encounter.

The Fatal Kiss

The ancient churchyard of Errigal Truagh in the townland of Mullanacross, in County Monaghan, Ireland is well known for its distinctively carved tombstones featuring images of skulls, bones, coffins and hourglasses. But visitors to the graveyard would do well to avoid lingering there by themselves and, should they fail to heed my warning, they would be well advised to shun any comely stranger they might encounter. For the graveyard of Errigal Truagh is said to be haunted by a malevolent spirit with whom an encounter is always fatal.

The nineteenth century writer and collector of Irish folklore, William Carleton, wrote of this spirit, "When a funeral takes place, it is said to watch the person who last remains in the graveyard, over whom it exercises a fascinating influence. If the person be a young man, it takes the shape of a beautiful female, inspires him with a charmed passion and exacts a promise that he will meet her in the churchyard one month from that day. This promise is sealed with a kiss that communicates a deadly taint to the individual who receives it. The spirit then disappears and no sooner does the individual from whom it received the promise and the kiss pass the boundary of the churchyard than he remembers the history of the specter — which is well known in the parish, sinks into despair and insanity, dies and is buried in the place of the appointment on the day when the promise was to have been fulfilled. If, on the contrary, it appears to a female, it assumes the form of a young man of exceeding elegance and beauty.

"I was shown the grave of a young person about eighteen years of age who it was said about four months before to have fallen victim to it;" Carleton continues, "and not many months previously a man in the same parish declared that he gave the promise and the fatal kiss and consequentially looked upon himself as lost. He took a fever, died and was buried on the day appointed for the meeting, which was exactly a month from that of the interview. Incredible as it may appear, the friends of these two persons solemnly declared that the particulars of the meeting were detailed repeatedly by the two persons without the slightest variation.

"There are several cases of the same kind mentioned, but the two now alluded to are the only ones that came within my personal knowledge. It appears, however, that the specter does not confine its operations to the churchyard only as there have been instances mentioned of its appearance at weddings and dances, where it never fails to secure its victims by dancing them into pleuritic fevers."

The Holy Island of Monaincha

I, myself, had an unnerving experience one morning in 2013 while wandering amidst the ancient graves and ominous stone burial vaults which populate the ruins of the small twelfth century Monaincha Abbey which encompasses almost all of the Holy Island of Monaincha on the outskirts of Roscrea, in County Tipperary, Ireland.

I had visited the abbey out of curiosity regarding a legend concerning the site. Although drained by the owner of the property in the 1790's, Monaincha was, for centuries, a place of pilgrimage surrounded by a bog. The twelfth century Norman clergyman and chronicler, Gerald of Wales, wrote that the island was called "The Isle of the living" and that it "has a chapel cared for most devotedly by a few celibates called 'heaven-worshippers'."

A thirteenth century Norwegian text called, *"The King's Mirror,"* stated:

"In that lake is an islet inhabited by men who live a celibate life and may be called, as one likes, either monks or hermits; they live there in such numbers that they fill the island, though at times they are fewer. It is said concerning this isle that it is healthful and quite free from diseases, so that people grow aged more slowly there than elsewhere in the land. But when one does grow very old and sickly and can see the end of the days allotted by the Lord, he has to be carried to some place on the mainland to die; for no one can die of disease on the island. One may sicken and suffer there, but his spirit cannot depart from the body before he has been removed from the island."

Over the centuries the ruins of the abbey and the rest of the island devolved into an eerie and somewhat macabre cemetery. Although I tend to feel highly uncomfortable in graveyards, always desiring to depart from them as quickly as possible, and although I was completely alone at the time; I found myself so intrigued by Monaincha that I found it almost impossible to leave. When, finally, I did decide to depart, every ounce of strength I possessed seemed to begin to drain from my body. I felt, if I did not immediately leave the island, I would pass out. This was very strange as I was in very good health at the time and I had gotten enough sleep the night before. I had, only an hour or so before, enjoyed a full Irish breakfast and I had felt extremely energetic while riding a bicycle approximately two and a half kilometers from my bed and breakfast to the abbey.

As what I can only call my "life-force" began to fade, I recalled legends I had read of supernatural entities taking people who had remained too long in a location under their control down into the realm of the "Otherworld." And, while I had never believed such tales, I suddenly became concerned and, though still feeling faint, I managed to summon up enough strength to, with some difficulty, make my way to the edge of where, centuries before, the bog had originally surrounded the island. The further I moved away from Monaincha, the better I felt until, finally, upon reaching what had been the far bank of what had once been the bog, I was back to feeling completely normal again.

After leaving Monaincha by way of the unpaved path which leads from a paved road to the island, I turned to the left and bicycled a kilometer or more up the paved road heading away from Roscrea, exploring the countryside.

Finally, I turned around and headed back toward Roscrea. When I neared the place where one could make a right-hand turn onto the path leading back to the island, the front wheel of my bicycle, seemingly of its own accord, turned and sent me heading back toward the island. This so alarmed me that I immediately yanked the handlebars back in the opposite direction and pedaled for all I was worth until I was far from the path which would have taken me back to Monaincha.

Is there some sinister force at Monaincha lying in wait for the unwary or was it all in my mind? I will never know for certain.

The Elemental in the Granary

Dermot MacManus, in *The Middle Kingdom*, recalls the evening, one summer day in his seventh year when he was returning with his father from the orchard on their family estate in Kiltimagh, County Mayo, Ireland. As twilight fell and shadows from the orchard lengthened, his father stopped, faced the orchard and, three times, made the sign of the cross in the air.

"Daddy, why did you do that?" the young boy asked.

After a moment's hesitation, his father answered in a solemn voice, "There are things there that it is better to keep at a distance."

It was only years later that MacManus' father told Dermot of an experience which occurred when he was around fourteen years old.

His father had been playing hide-and-go-seek one afternoon in and around the family stable buildings with his brother, Arthur, when, while hiding in the granary, he heard the sound of stamping hooves and frantic snorting in the stable twelve feet below him. Curious as to what was going on, he opened a trap door and looked down to see two terrified horses attempting to flee from a threatening "something" lurking near the manger.

Then the "thing" came into focus. He saw, as MacManus would later describe it, "something that filled him with horror — a sight that he never forgot all the days of his life. There crouched a figure of evil with baleful eyes, blazing red like coals of fire. It was huddled in a compact ball, as a boy of his own size might look when squatting on his haunches. It gripped the edge of the manger and was a dirty greyish-brown. The fingers were bone and sinew and ended not in human nails but in curved, pointed claws."

The boy slammed the trap door shut and fled the granary, frantically calling out for his brother in warning.

What MacManus' father had encountered may have been what is sometimes called an "elemental," an entity thought by some to be a nature spirit. In the words of the famous early twentieth century ghost hunter, Elliott O'Donnell, the elemental is "a species of the phantasm that has never inhabited any kind of earthly body."

The elemental could be, O'Donnell theorized, "a survival (or descendant) of the earliest attempts at life on this planet — possibly an experiment in forms of life half physical, half superphysical — prior to the creation and selection of animal and vegetable life as it is known to us."

The Leap Castle Elemental

Perhaps the most famous entity to be labeled an elemental is the horrific creature which is said to haunt Leap Castle in County Offaly, Ireland. Built around 1250, the castle has long been called "The Most Haunted Castle in Ireland." The most fearsome of the numerous supernatural entities said to dwell within the castle or on its grounds, is the creature known as "It" or "The Elemental."

Mildred Darby who lived in the Castle along with her husband, Jonathan, until it was largely destroyed by fire in 1922, encountered "The Elemental" at least three times.

"I was standing in the Gallery looking down at the main floor when I felt somebody put a hand on my shoulder," she wrote. "The thing was about the size of a sheep. Thin, gaunt, shadowy ... its face was human, to be more accurate, inhuman. ... eyes, which seemed half decomposed in black cavities, stared into mine. The horrible smell one hundred times intensified came up into my face, giving me a deadly nausea. It was the smell of a decomposing corpse."

She was to later describe another encounter with "It" in a letter to a friend. This time her husband, who always vehemently denied that his home was in any way haunted, saw "It" as well.

"On the 25th November 1915," she disclosed, "two of our servants knowing the 'master' would be late and that I was driving that afternoon had invited 'friends,' two soldiers from the Barracks at Birr distant the other side six miles. They came rather late and my husband came home early so the visitors had to be kept out of his sight in the lower regions of one of the wings and were unable to be shown the centre tower — the very lofty hall.

"At 7:15 my husband and I went up to dress for dinner, my room in extremity of house from kitchens, his dressing room next door to me.

"Whilst dressing I was startled by a loud yell of terror stricken male and female voices coming apparently from the hall — and ran out to see the cause. My husband was out ahead of me at his heels. I passed through corridor of the wing and onto the gallery ....

"On the gallery leaning with 'hands' resting on its rail I saw the Thing — the Elemental and smelt it only too well. At the same moment my husband pulled up sharply about ten feet from the Thing, and half turning let fly a volley of abuse at me ending up: 'Dressing up a thing like that to try and make a fool of me. And now you'll say I've seen something and I have not seen anything and there is nothing to see, or ever was.' This last speech without a pause, begun (by) waving one hand at the Thing, end(ed) up by stalking back to his dressing room still abusing me for trying to give him a fright. As he was speaking the Elemental grew fainter and fainter in its outlines until it disappeared. ... He never made any enquiry as to the yell that called us both out, and from that day to this has not mentioned the incident to me.

"I heard from our servants that when we went to dress for dinner they had brought their friends just to show them the hall, when all four had suddenly seen and smelt the Elemental looking down at them from the gallery. They all got such a turn, they couldn't help letting out a bawl then fled to servants quarters where all four were very sick."

The next day the two maids presented Mrs. Darby with letters claiming it was necessary for them to immediately pay visits to their homes. They never returned to Leap.

Yet another encounter with "The Elemental" was recounted in a letter from a former houseguest to Mildred Darby.

"You have asked me to write down just what happened last night when you, with my brother and myself, had just come in from listening to the dogs making a tremendous barking and howling at half past eleven," wrote the houseguest.

"When we came into the big hall I had my arm round your waist, and it was a sudden start that you gave made me look at your face.

"I saw your eyes fixed upon something above our heads, and the next minute my own eyes were filled by the sight of a Thing in the gallery looking down at us. There was plenty of light from the lamps in the hall, and the one above on the wall at the corner of the gallery, for every one of us to see quite plainly the grey-colored figure about the height of a small grown-up person looking down at us.

"I wish I thought I could ever forget the sight of that grey figure with dark spots like holes in its head instead of eyes, standing with grey arms folded on the gallery railing looking down at us. It was the cry I gave in my horror made my brother look up too, and without waiting a second you remember he said, 'Stand here you two, and I will run round and upstairs to the gallery just to see who that joker is. I'll teach him to dress up like that to try and give you ladies a fright.'

"You and I stood just where we were, and neither of us said a word. Our eyes were fixed on the Thing — at least I know mine were and never shifted. I heard the rushing footsteps of my brother as he ran upstairs, and the opening of the gallery door. Then just as he put foot on the gallery, the Thing that he saw there, that we were watching, suddenly faded out of sight. The Thing did not move, only became less and less visible, until it vanished.

"My brother searched the gallery for any trace or sign of the figure we had all three seen, but found nothing.

"I only wish you would come away with us today. I do not like leaving you in this weird place, where I personally could not summon courage to remain another night."

Can Ghosts Be Photographed?

I am often asked if a ghost can be photographed. From the very advent of photography, charlatans and hoaxers have produced hundreds, if not thousands, of spurious "ghost photographs." And while it is impossible to completely exclude the possibility of fraud or a, yet to be discovered, "natural" explanation, in what appears to be an actual photograph of a ghost, occasionally, a photograph emerges which withstands the careful scrutiny of modern investigative techniques. Here are four photographs which I feel pass that test.

The Brown Lady of Raynham Hall

Our first, possibly authentic, ghost photograph involves "The Brown Lady" of Raynham Hall, one of the great country houses of England. Dating back almost 400 years, Raynham Hall is said to be haunted by Lady Dorothy Walpole, who, in 1713, married Charles Townshend, the 2nd Viscount Townshend, a man said to have had a violent temper;

a temper which was roused even more than usual when he heard gossip to the effect that his wife once had an amorous liaison with the notorious Lord Thomas Wharton, a man whose character was said to be so infamous that no young woman could withstand twenty-four hours under his roof without damage to her reputation.

Charles, it is claimed, punished his wife for her indiscretion, real or imaginary, by imprisoning Dorothy in her rooms in Raynham Hall until her death in 1726. While it was said that she died from smallpox, some claimed she was thrown down a staircase.

The first known sighting of Dorothy's ghost occurred during an 1835 Christmas gathering hosted by the then Lord and Lady Townshend who had recently inherited Raynham Hall. Two of their guests, a Colonel Loftus and a man named Hawkins, encountered the ghost on the way to their bedrooms. According to Colonel Loftus, she was wearing an old-fashioned brown satin gown similar to that seen in a portrait of Lady Dorothy which hung in one of the bedrooms. The ghost's cadaverous face glowed phosphorescently in the darkness of the hallway and, Loftus observed only dark, empty, cavernous holes where her eyes should be.

The Colonel quickly decided to leave Raynham Hall earlier than planned as did other guests who either observed the ghost themselves or did not wish to take the chance of such an unwelcome encounter. Some of the servants quickly departed as well.

Lord Townshend was understandably upset over this and called upon his friend, the novelist, Captain Frederick Marryat, a man well known for his having demonstrated extreme bravery during his twenty-four years of service in the British Navy.

As recorded by his daughter Florence, Captain Marryat was "indignant at the trick he believed had been played upon him. There was a great deal of smuggling and poaching in Norfolk at that period, as he knew well, being a magistrate of the county, and he felt sure that some of these depredators were trying to frighten the Townshends away from the Hall.

"So he asked his friends to let him stay with them and sleep in the haunted chamber, and he felt sure he could rid them of the nuisance. They accepted his offer, and he took possession of the room in which the portrait of the apparition hung, and in which she had been often seen, and slept each night with a loaded revolver under his pillow. For two days, however, he saw nothing, and the third was to be the limit of his stay.

"On the third night, however, two young men (nephews of the baronet) knocked at his door as he was undressing to go to bed, and asked him to step over to their room (which was at the other end of the corridor), and give them his opinion of a new gun just arrived from London. My father was in his shirt and trousers, but as the hour was late, and everybody had retired to rest except themselves, he prepared to accompany them as he was. As they were leaving the room, he caught up his revolver, 'in case we meet the Brown Lady,' he said, laughing.

"When the inspection of the gun was over, the young men in the same spirit declared they would accompany my father back again, 'in case you meet the Brown Lady,' they repeated, laughing also. The three gentlemen therefore returned in company. The corridor was long and dark, for the lights had been extinguished, but as they reached the middle of it, they saw the glimmer of a lamp coming towards them from the other end. "One of the ladies going to visit the nurseries," whispered the young Townshends to my father.

"Now, the bedroom doors in that corridor faced each other, and each room had a double door with a space between, as is the case in many old-fashioned country houses. My father (as I have said) was in a shirt and trousers only, and his native modesty made him feel uncomfortable, so he slipped within one of the outer doors (his friends following his example), in order to conceal himself until the lady should have passed by.

"I have heard him describe how he watched her approaching nearer and nearer, through the chink of the door, until, as she was close enough for him to distinguish the colors and style of her costume, he recognized the figure as the facsimile of the portrait of 'The Brown Lady.' He had his finger on the trigger of his revolver, and was about to demand it to stop and give the reason for its presence there, when the figure halted of its own accord before the door behind which he stood, and, holding the lighted lamp she carried to her features, deliberately grinned at him.

"This act so infuriated my father, who was anything but lamb-like in disposition, that he sprang into the corridor with a bound, and discharged the revolver right in her face. The figure instantly disappeared — the figure at which for the space of several minutes three men had been looking together — and the bullet passed through the outer door of the room on the opposite side of the corridor and lodged in the panel of the inner door. My father never attempted again to interfere with the Brown Lady, and I have heard that she haunts the premises to this day."

Among the other guests who have encountered the "Brown Lady" over the years was King George IV who observed her standing by his bed.

In 1936 a photographer, Captain Hubert C. Provand, and his assistant, Indre Shira, were sent by the British magazine, *Country Life*, to photograph Raynham Hall for an article on the house.

After photographing various parts of the house, at around four in the afternoon, they took a photograph of the oak staircase. As Provand refocused his camera in preparation for a second shot, Shira excitedly shouted, "Quick! Quick! There's something! Are you ready?"

"Yes," Provand replied as he removed the camera's lens cap and Shira pushed the trigger on his flash gun.

Upon closing the shutter and emerging from under his focusing cloth, Provand asked, "What's all the excitement about?"

Shira explained that he had seen "an ethereal, veiled form coming slowly down the stairs."

Provand laughed and said that Shira must have merely imagined that he had seen something.

Shira bet Provand five pounds that, when the negative was developed, it would show something of a supernatural nature. He won his bet for the finished print did, indeed, show a filmy, ghostly form descending the staircase.

The famed English ghost investigator, Harry Price, interviewed both Shira and Provand and, after thoroughly examining the negative, Price came to the conclusion that it had neither been faked nor was there some "natural" explanation for the image on the staircase.

Since that time, critics have put forth theories from the phantom figure being the result of a shaken camera, to the photographers having smeared grease on the negative, to the photograph being a double exposure utilizing a statue of the Virgin Mary.

My opinion is that these criticisms fall far short of proving the photograph to be a fraud and, perhaps, the final word should be given to Lord Charles Townshend, the current owner and resident of Raynham Hall, who has stated, "No one has proved the picture taken of her is a fake. She isn't there to haunt the house but she is still there. I know she's there and I'm glad she's around."

The Brown Lady of Raynham Hall

The Ghost on the Tulip Staircase

An equally famous photograph also involves a ghost on a staircase. In 1966, the Reverend R. W. Hardy, a retired Canadian clergyman, and his wife were touring the Queen's House at the National Maritime Museum in Greenwich, England when he took a photograph of its celebrated Tulip Staircase.

As no one was on the staircase at the time, when the photograph was developed, the Hardys were surprised to see the ghost-like figure of a hooded figure climbing the staircase. Mystified, Hardy, who had no previous interest in the paranormal, sent the original color transparency to the venerable and highly regarded Ghost Club in England where it was thoroughly examined both by them and photographic experts at Kodak who were unable to find any evidence or fraud or a double exposure.

Upon further investigation, Peter Underwood, the president of The Ghost Club and the author of numerous books on the subject of ghosts, found that a former employee of the museum had, on several occasions, seen unexplainable figures in the vicinity of the staircase and that one of the Warders at the Queen's House had heard footsteps there for which he could not account. Others have, over the years, spoken of being touched by an invisible "something" and of hearing children's voices singing there.

In 1967, the Ghost Club carried out a carefully controlled all-night investigation of the Queen's House. Although no apparitions were seen or photographed, such unexplainable sounds as "the single peal of a bell" and "the sounds of muttering, crying and footsteps were heard."

As recently as 2002, Tony Anderson, a gallery assistant at the Queen's House, while talking with two other staff members, heard a door close and saw a ghostly figure attired in a grey or white crinoline dress glide across the balcony on the top floor before floating away through a wall. All three of them rushed into the bedroom into which the phantom had vanished only to see it pass through an antechamber and, again, disappear through a wall. Each witness experienced a sudden shock of cold as they observed the ghost.

I agree with Peter Underwood who concluded, that this photograph "if genuine, is probably the best spontaneous ghost photograph in existence."

The Ghost on the Tulip Staircase

The Kneeling Ghost

In 1966, Gordon Carroll, a, then, eighteen-year-old amateur photographer, who was taking colored slides of the stained glass windows in the thirteenth century church of St. Mary the Virgin in Woodford, Northhamptonshire, England, took an extraordinary photograph.

Although there had been no one else in the church at the time he had taken the photograph, after sending his film off for developing, Carroll was shocked to find something he had not expected in a shot he had taken of the church altar. Kneeling before the altar was the ghost-like form of a figure which appears to be a monk or, perhaps, a medieval knight wearing a white or light colored surplice or tabard.

A soft-spoken, devout Catholic who had taken thousand of photographs of old houses, castles and churches over the previous two to three years, Carroll told a reporter for *The People* newspaper, which first published the photograph, that he had taken the photograph with an Ilford Sportsman Rangefinder camera using Agfa C.T. 18 film in the course of taking a few other photographs in the church.

After sending the film off to be processed and receiving the finished slides, Carroll was surprised to find, in one of them, the unexpected phantom image.

When asked if the young man could have perpetrated a hoax of some kind, Father Crawford, Carroll's parish priest, responded forcefully, that Carroll was not the kind of person who would do anything of that nature.

Furthermore, after being warned that if he gave a false statement under oath he could be prosecuted for perjury, Carroll attested to all of the facts concerning the photograph before a Commissioner of Oaths.

After examining the slide, an expert with Agfa stated, "There has been no trick photography used in taking this film. There has been no double exposure. There is no flaw in the actual film or fault in the developing it. I would stake my reputation on that."

The image of a phantom in the photograph should not come as a complete surprise as the Church of St. Mary the Virgin has long been known to both be haunted and to harbor a macabre secret.

During the course of making repairs to the church in the spring of 1866, a small recess in the north side of the nave was revealed. Inside this recess they discovered, within a wicker box, a bundle of coarse cloth. Upon unwrapping the cloth, they found a mummified human heart!

Many years ago, a woman told of how, while in the church making an arrangement of wildflowers, she was stunned to see the ghostly figure of a monk make its way to the altar where it then knelt in prayer. She fled the church in terror. When she returned in the company of the parish priest, the ghost had vanished.

Another woman stated that, while alone in the church, she had encountered the same phantom. But, instead of kneeling in prayer, this time the monk made its way up the aisle towards her only to vanish at the place where the mummified heart had been found.

There have been reports of others encountering the ghost in recent times as well.

The Kneeling Ghost

224

The Holbrooke Hotel Ghost

As stated in earlier chapters, the Holbrooke Hotel in Grass Valley, California has been the site of numerous examples of ghostly activity.

In 2010 I was asked to appear in an episode of the television program, *My Ghost Story*, concerning an intriguing photograph which had been taken by Mary Moore who, along with her husband, Gary, had checked into the Holbrooke for a short stay.

Enchanted by the hotel's Gold Rush era architecture, Mary began to take a number of photographs with her simple automatic camera using ordinary still photography film.

A member of the hotel staff suggested to her that she might find the large iron doors in the basement to be of particular interest, these being the highly secure doors through which, it has been said, gold shipments from Grass Valley's gold mines once flowed. Upon her attempting to photograph one of the iron doors, the lens of her camera unexpectedly began zooming in and out by itself and she experienced the inescapable sensation that some invisible presence was standing directly behind her.

Frightened, she immediately fled back upstairs. As Mary had heard that the ghost of a woman in turn of the last century dress was sometimes observed ascending the staircase to the second floor, she took a photograph from the second floor landing.

When the Moores returned to their home in Southern California they had the photographs Mary had taken developed and printed. To their surprise, they discovered what appeared to be a ghost clearly visible in the photograph she had taken from the second floor landing. Appearing behind the right-hand center windowpane was the form of a man visible from only his waist upwards.

It could not have been the reflection of anyone on the landing as Mary, who had taken the photograph, is not seen reflected in the photograph. Furthermore, she had not seen the man in the window at the time she snapped the shutter and it would have been physically impossible for any living person to have been standing behind the window in the position seen in the photograph.

In the course of filming the *My Ghost Story* episode I had the pleasure of getting to know Mary, to hear her story directly from her and to examine her camera. As a result, I have absolutely no doubt as to the authenticity of the photograph. And, upon carefully examining the place from which the photograph was taken, I have come to the conclusion that there is no "natural" explanation for the figure seen in the window.

The Holbrooke Hotel Ghost

Close-up of the Holbrooke Hotel Photograph

228

How to Investigate a Haunting

Before we enter into a discussion of how to best investigate an alleged haunting, a discussion of how to find a haunting to investigate is in order. Unless you are lucky enough to have someone bring a particular haunting to your attention, you will need to do some research.

If you live in a large city the odds are good that one or more books will have been written on the subject of ghosts said to haunt the geographic region in which you live. Ask your librarian or local bookstore staff if he or she can suggest an appropriate book.

Search for books on regional legends as well. Although in many cases the stories in such books may be just that, legends; there may be a germ of truth in one or more of the stories which might be worth exploring further.

While you are at the library, ask if they have a file containing clippings of newspaper and magazine articles concerning local ghost stories. Your local newspaper might have such a file in their "morgue" which, if you ask in a business-like manner, they might be willing to share with you.

An online search might yield surprising results as well. Just put the name of your town and state along with such keywords as "ghost," "haunted," "supernatural" and "legend" into a search engine and follow up on any and all search results which might come up.

You might also search the internet in the hope of finding a local paranormal research group you might join. If no such local group exits, you might consider starting one yourself.

If, after all of this, you have still "come up empty," do not despair. At this point you will need to take matters into your own hands and ask everyone you can if they might be aware of a local haunting.

It was at the suggestion of a friend that eighteen years ago I set out in search of local ghost stories in my hometown of Nevada City, California. "Someone should give a Nevada City ghost tour," she suggested following a conversation in which I had mentioned having enjoyed a fascinating historical ghost walk while performing in Victoria, British Columbia.

The idea appealed to me as I had, for years, been relating true accounts of haunting on scores of television and radio programs and, many years before, I had taught a university course on parapsychological topics.

But were there, I wondered, actually enough Nevada City hauntings to warrant a public tour? I had read an account of ghostly activity having occurred at our county historical society's museum and I had heard rumors of a Nevada City bed and breakfast inn being haunted but that was all, hardly enough to justify an entire tour.

Delving into a folder of newspaper and magazine clippings at our county's historical research library, I unearthed a few promising accounts and, thus encouraged, I began to ask Nevada City store and restaurant proprietors, "Has anything strange, anything which you cannot account for in the way of a 'natural' explanation, ever occurred in your building?"

I was amazed by how often the person to whom I posed my query would respond, "How did you know?" or would reply, "Not in my building but ask next door. They'll tell you a story you won't believe!" And soon I had compiled more than enough accounts of haunted sites in Nevada City to create a proper tour.

Even more surprising was the fact that people then began coming to me sharing their own first-hand accounts of local hauntings.

It was not long before I was asked to research and conduct a historical ghost tour of the neighboring town of Grass Valley. This tour resulted in so many more people sharing stories of their local paranormal encounters with me that I eventually found I had collected enough stories to write an entire book on the subject of Nevada City and Grass Valley ghosts.

As my experience suggests, it is often productive to ask everyone you know if they are aware of any potential hauntings. You might be amazed by the number of people you know who have had a paranormal experience but have been reluctant to tell anyone about it.

A 1973 survey in the United Kingdom found that one out of every five Britons who were asked said that they had experienced a paranormal event of some kind in their lifetime and one in every ten disclosed that they had encountered a ghost.

You might also consider requesting, through a local Facebook group page or one of the many online groups devoted to the subject of ghosts and related paranormal phenomena, that anyone who believes they have experienced a haunting in your area contact you.

Another approach might be to investigate a home in which a small child claims to have what is usually dismissed an "imaginary friend."

The English parapsychologist, Andrew Green, once carried out a study which suggests both that young children might possess psychic abilities which society gradually trains out of them and that their imaginary friends might not always be imaginary after all. Green interviewed one hundred and twenty-five children, aged six to twelve. Slightly over half of the children interviewed, sixty-five, "described human figures that they had seen, in some cases several times, but which were not apparently visible to their parents. Twenty-seven out of sixty-five descriptions were found to match those of people who had once occupied the child's current home."

"Unfortunately," Green added, "I was unable to establish if more than nine of the twenty-seven people described were deceased."

While I was fortunate in that I live in an area which dates back over a hundred and seventy years to the California Gold Rush and, thus, my region has had time to accumulate more haunting than might be found in a more modern city or town, diligent research can unearth a wealth of hauntings and other paranormal events in almost every vicinity. Modern cities and new homes are often built on land upon which earlier civilizations, such as the Native Americans in North America, may have lived and died for prior centuries. That being the case, it is not unusual for a ghost from an earlier era to be encountered in a new house which was built upon the site of an earlier dwelling or which was the site of an event likely to create a haunting.

Accounts of hauntings can be found everywhere and, with a little persistence you will almost certainly find one or more cases to investigate.

Anniversary Ghosts

Perhaps you might be so fortunate as to live in or near an area in which an anniversary ghost is said to be seen. An anniversary ghost is a ghost which is said to appear each year, on a particular date. Famous examples of anniversary ghosts include phantom monks said to haunt the ruins of Glastonbury Abbey in England each January 6th and the ghost of Lady Jane Grey which is said to appear as a "white shape" near the Bloody Tower at the Tower of London each February 12th, the anniversary of her beheading on Tower Green in 1554.

However, a problem arises with any anniversary ghost believed to have first appeared prior to 1582 when the world, gradually over the course of three hundred years, changed from the Julian to the Gregorian calendar. In 1582, this change resulted in Italy, Poland, Portugal, Spain and most of France dropping ten days from their calendars. From 1583 to 1700, in different years, Austria, Hungary and regions of Germany each dropped ten days from their calendars. In 1752 most of what would become the United States and Canada and the United Kingdom and her colonies dropped eleven days from their calendars. In 1872 through 1873 Japan dropped twelve days from their calendars. And during the years 1916 through 1927, in different years, Bulgaria, Estonia, Russia, Greece and Turkey all dropped thirteen days from their calendars.

So in order to properly investigate an anniversary ghost which first appeared prior to 1582, one might consider visiting the site of the haunting both on the traditional date of the haunting and on a date ten to thirteen days later depending upon the country involved. For instance, you would add eleven days to the anniversary date of a pre-1752 ghost in the United States, Canada, the United Kingdom or Ireland.

And, making things more complicated still, even in the case of more recent haunting, there is the issue of leap year which occurs almost, but not always, every four years.

In the hope of avoiding the problem of a leap year, when, in 1974, I visited Marie Antoinette's Hamlet and the grounds of the Trianon palaces at Versailles, I spent the entire days of August 9th, August 10th (the traditional date of the haunting) and August 11th in the areas of the Hamlet and the Trianons which were said to be haunted. And, still, I encountered nothing which could be considered to be proof of a haunting on any of those three dates.

However, as the Versailles case illustrates, the fact that a ghost has been said to haunt a particular location on a particular date is not a guarantee of witnessing an apparition. Another parapsychological researcher with whom I have discussed this case visited the Hamlet and the Trianons every year on August 10th for a number of years and, with the exception of one visit during which he experienced, for only a few moments, what Charlotte Anne Moberly described as an unnatural, flat, two dimensional look to the landscape, he experienced nothing else of a paranormal nature on any of his yearly visits.

The fact that, when Eleanor Jourdain revisited the Versailles grounds on January 2nd of the following year, she experienced ghostly encounters similar those which she and Miss Moberly had experienced on August 10th, along with ghostly encounters by others at Versailles on dates other than the 10th of August, makes me wonder whether apparitions believed to appear on one specific date are actually there throughout the entire year but are usually only sought out and, therefore, only occasionally seen on the one traditional date.

Still, should you live in the United Kingdom and wish to investigate an anniversary ghost, Peter Underwood's extremely insightful and useful book, *The Ghost Hunter's Guide*, lists seventeen pages of the dates and locations of anniversary ghosts in Britain. And his book, *Ghosts and How to See Them*, lists several more anniversary ghosts throughout the world.

Interviewing the Witnesses

Once you have chosen the haunting you will be investigating, you will begin your preliminary research by interviewing the witnesses to the alleged haunting. If there are more than one witness you will want to interview each witness separately so that the testimony of one witness does not influence the testimony of the other witnesses. Although this testimony may be written down in a notebook, if the witness agrees, it is easiest and the most accurate to record such testimony via a tape recorder or any other recording device you might have.

If possible, these interviews should take place at the site of the ghostly encounter so that you can draw a map of the area in which an apparition was seen or, in the case of a poltergeist, objects were observed to have moved. On this map you will indicate the position of both the apparition and the witness, noting the direction the witness was facing when he or she saw the apparition.

You should think of yourself as being a reporter asking such questions as when did the event occur? How long did the paranormal experience last?

Ask each witness for as complete a description of the apparition as possible. Describing an apparition as being short or tall tells us very little as a figure which appears tall to a child may appear to be of normal height to an adult. Perhaps the witness can clarify the apparition's size by comparing it to something present at the site.

The same need for precise details is necessary when a witness describes the ghost's manner of dress. A phrase such as "old-fashioned clothing" could mean anything from the clothing of nineteen fifties to Victorian attire to that of the Renaissance or to a time even earlier.

If the apparition was seen more than once, ask if there is any pattern to its movements and actions. Does it follow the same path and do exactly the same thing over and over again each time it is seen or were its movements and actions different each time it was observed?

Ask if the witness had any previous knowledge of the history of the haunted site.

Does the witness have any vision problems? If so, was the witness wearing his or her glasses at the time he or she observed the ghost? Is the witness colorblind?

Were there any animals present at the time of the sighting? If so, did they react in any unusual manner?

If the witness heard a door open or close did he or she check to see if the door actually opened or closed or was it merely the sound of a door being opened or closed which was heard? The same kind of question should be asked with regard to water inexplicably flowing from a water faucet. Did the faucet handle actually turn by itself to the open position?

If footsteps were heard, were they light or heavy?

If a tapping sound was heard, try to determine the exact nature of the sound. Was it, perhaps, a light taping such as a bird might make on a window or heaving tapping such as that made by a wooden cane as one walks across a hardwood floor?

If a fragrance or odor is detected try to have the witness compare it to another common smell.

Was the apparition seen in a mirror?

If the apparition is seen or heard within a building, ask if there are any hidden chambers or other unseen features in the building.

Other Preliminary Research

Your next step will take you back to the library to see if you can find anything about the historical background of the haunted site. Perhaps the site was the scene of a violent act which might have produced a ghost. However, the fact that someone died in a particular house or on a particular piece of property, rarely, by itself, produces a haunting. If you are investigating an old and well known house, you might find valuable information in a file your library may keep containing newspaper clippings regarding important houses in the area.

If you live in the United Kingdom and can obtain an ordinance map of the site, you might discover caves, tunnels or underground water channels which could provide a natural explanation to what might otherwise appear to be paranormal phenomena. Unfortunately, equivalent maps of this type are rare in the United States.

Your Basic Ghost Hunting Equipment

Although some investigators invest in a large number of expensive pieces of equipment, in my opinion, this is completely unnecessary. The basic assortment of equipment you will need to bring with you for your onsite investigation of the haunting consists of the following:

An adequate supply of pens or pencils

A notebook in which you will record your observations

Graph paper upon which you will draw the floor plan of a haunted room or a map of an outdoor site
A tape measure for, in the case of a poltergeist, measuring the distance an object may have moved or, in the case of an apparition, the distance from the observer to the ghost

A camera (preferably with a sturdy tripod)

An audio recording device for recording unexpected and, possibly, paranormal noises

Spare batteries for any electrical equipment you might be bringing with you as batteries have often been known to unexpectedly and quickly die in haunted locations

Sticks of chalk for outlining the position of objects which might move of their own accord

A spool of thread

"Museum" or "earthquake" putty or some other nondestructive adhesive to secure the ends of thread which is stretched across an open area through which the ghost is alleged to pass

Nondestructive tape which, along with a length of thread, is used to seal off doors

Flour which can be lightly spread onto a floor to detect human or animal footprints

Sugar which can also be spread onto a floor to provide a crunching sound should a human or animal walk upon it

Walkie-Talkies or cell phones

A tote bag, attaché case, backpack or small suitcase in which to store your ghost hunting equipment

Optional Equipment

An inexpensive compass

Some investigators claim that the presence of a ghost will cause the compass needle, which under normal conditions points to magnetic north, to move about erratically. There may be many factors which could be the reason for such movements and there is no scientific evidence to suggest that ghosts cause compass needles to move. However, as a compass can be cheaply obtained and can be used in other situations, it might be worth bringing one along in order to see for yourself if a ghost can, indeed, affect a compass should you be so fortunate as to observe an apparition in close proximity to where you have placed the compass.

An indoor/outdoor thermometer

For centuries ghosts have been said to cause a sudden drop in the temperature. It has been suggested that a ghost absorbs the heat in the air around it. Again, there is no scientific evidence for this. I suspect that the notion of ghosts creating "cold spots" may have originated from imagining a corpse lying in a cold grave.

While I have often felt a sudden chill when investigating an alleged haunting, it is impossible to know whether this is due merely to the expectation of encountering a ghost or if one's body is somehow reacting to an unconscious awareness of an unseen entity in the same way that you can sometimes sense the unseen arrival of a living person behind you.

Still, should you already have a digital indoor/outdoor thermometer or a sixteen inch or taller garden thermometer which can be easily read, at a distance, you might bring it along in your kit. If, as in the case of the compass, you are able to read a sudden drop in the temperature at the same time you see an apparition, you will have proved that there may, indeed, be a connection between the two events.

An infrared/ultraviolet full spectrum camera

While, as of yet, there is no scientific proof that the image of a ghost can be more easily caught through full spectrum photography than with a normal camera, some researchers believe that this is an area worth exploring. And, as relatively inexpensive, previously used digital cameras in which all of the blocking filters have been removed can be obtained on online sites such as Ebay, full spectrum photography at locations said to be haunted might be worth pursuing.

On June 29, 2021 I took several infrared/full spectrum photographs of the Bourn Cottage on the grounds of the Empire Mine in Grass Valley, California.

The Empire Mine, in operation from 1869 to 1956, was one of the oldest, deepest and richest gold mines in California, producing 5.8 million troy ounces of gold. Now the Empire Mine Historic State Park, there are many who claim that the Bourn Cottage which mine owner, William Bowers Bourn Jr. had built on the property from mine rock to use as a summer home is haunted.

Docents working in the Cottage have spoken of creaking floorboards and cold drafts which defy any logical explanation and of feeling a ghostly presence in the house, perhaps, William Bourn Jr., himself; his wife, Agnes Moody Bourn; or, to my mind, more likely, Katie Moriarty, the Irish housekeeper and caretaker who, from the year 1900 until her retirement in 1943, ran the house with such supreme efficiency that she still found the time to bake cookies for the children in the Sisters of Mercy's orphanage in Grass Valley.

It is said that the image of a woman in late Victorian or Edwardian clothing appeared in a photograph which was taken in the Cottage many years ago. Although, upon hearing of this, I tried to track down the photograph or to find anyone who recalled actually seeing it, the photograph has yet to be found.

As the Cottage was locked and unoccupied at the time of my most recent visit, I decide to take a number of photographs of the exterior of the Cottage with my infrared/full spectrum camera. Although I saw nothing unusual at the time I took the photographs, upon later examination, I found what appears to be a face in the right-hand section of a second story window.

Did I capture the image of a ghost in the photograph on the next page or is it merely an optical artifact of some kind? I leave it to you to decide.

A Window of the Bourn Cottage

Pseudoscientific Ghost Hunting Devices

Due in large part to the popularity of television shows in which self-described "ghost busters" purport to investigate haunted locations with pseudoscientific devices, an industry has developed offering an assortment of often expensive ghost hunting tools and gadgets which range from those having unproven investigative value to those which are completely fraudulent. Here are three devices which, in my opinion, are a complete waste of your time and money.

Electromagnet Field Detectors
also known as "Ghost Meters"

These handheld meters are designed to detect what their proponents term EMFs; fluctuations in the electromagnetic field. And, while these meters do exactly what they are intended to do, the problems inherent in using an EMF meter in order to detect ghosts are twofold.

First, the value of the EMF readings relies entirely upon the assumption that ghosts emit electromagnetism, an assumption for which there is absolutely no scientific proof.

Second, even if it were true that ghosts emit an electromagnetic field, so do cell phones, cameras, walkie-talkies, flashlights and every other electronic device you may have with you as well as the electric wiring in a building's walls. Even the oscillation of a stationary piece of metal furniture which begins to imperceptivity vibrate due to nearby footsteps or the closing of a door will project an electromagnetic field. With all of these competing sources of EMF readings, how could one ever determine that the EMF being detected by the meter is coming from a ghost?

To make matters worse, there are devices on the market which have been preprogrammed to, upon detecting an electromagnetic fluctuation, speak one or more words in a ghostly voice; leading the unsophisticated user to believe an unseen entity is speaking to him!

Thermo Graphic Cameras
and
Infrared Thermometers

While these instruments will, indeed, show changes in temperature, as mentioned before in regard to the use of thermometers, there is no scientific evidence proving that ghosts cause "cold spots" or can cause changes in the temperature.

Making these devices of even less value to a paranormal investigation is the fact that they will only record the temperature of the visible, physical surface at which they have been aimed, such as a wall, rather than the ghost which might be imagined to be standing between the investigator and the wall.

An Onsite Experiment

As discussed earlier, animals often seem to be more aware of ghosts than you or I. This was illustrated by an experience which occurred at the Holbrooke Hotel where, many years ago, guests were allowed to have dogs stay with them in their rooms. On one occasion a guest assigned to Room 9, which many believe to be the most haunted room in the hotel, found that his dog became extremely agitated as he attempted to enter the room. The frightened dog whined and simply refused cross over the threshold.

If you are investigating a haunting in a house or other building in which one particular room is said to be where the ghost or ghostly activity has been observed, and, if the owner of the property will allow you to bring a well-behaved dog inside the premises, you might consider conducting the following experiment.

Instruct an assistant who has no knowledge of the details of the haunting to slowly take the dog on a leash from room to room throughout the building, asking the assistant to write down any reactions the dog might have as it enters and remains for a short period of time in each of the rooms.

It is crucial that your assistant be given no idea as to which room is believed to be the center of the alleged ghostly phenomena, as he might, through subtle, unconscious physical movements or his facial expression, communicate to the dog his knowledge as to where the ghost might be.

No one who has any knowledge whatsoever about the haunting should accompany the assistant and the dog as they move from room to room as that person could inadvertently influence the dog's behavior as well.

If the dog shows fear or agitation in the room which is said to be haunted, while not scientific proof, it would be evidence strongly suggesting that the indicated room may, indeed, be haunted.

If the experiment is repeated with another dog and another assistant (who is likewise uninformed as to both the details of the haunting and the results of the previous experiment) and this second dog reacts in the same way as the first in the same room, the evidence will be stronger still.

Although dogs seem to be the most sensitive to ghosts, this experiment might be attempted with a cat or other small animal as well.

Safety Issues

Although I am unaware of even one authentic case in which someone was harmed by a ghost, the serious ghost hunter should always follow a number of commonsense safety measures.

Do not investigate a haunting alone. Always have at least one other person with you who can contact emergency personnel in the case of an accident. If you are under eighteen years old, I would strongly advise you to have a parent, guardian or other responsible adult with you.

Let a responsible adult know where you will be going and when you expect to return home.

Never investigate a haunting in a dangerous neighborhood. As the old saying goes, "The dead ones can't hurt you. It's the live ones you have to watch out for!"

If you are investigating an abandoned building or a secluded outdoor site, notify the local law enforcement agency of your plans well ahead of time and, in the case of private property, show them that you have written permission from the property owner to carry out your investigation. Otherwise, your investigation might be unexpectedly interrupted by police officers and squad cars with flashing lights.

If you are working at night, I strongly suggest that you carry out your investigation with the lights on.

Despite the iconic motion picture image of the intrepid ghost hunter waiting in the dark for an unseen entity to make contact, there is absolutely no evidence to suggest that ghosts appear more often in the dark of night than in broad daylight or in a brightly illuminated room. Stumbling about an unfamiliar location in the dark is almost asking for a serious accident to occur. And, if you do see an apparition or experience poltergeist activity, doing so in full light will allow you to observe details which will add more credibility to your observation and it will counter any suggestion that you misinterpreted some animal or other physical object which was seen only hazily or indistinctly in the darkness.

What Kind of Ghost Are You Investigating?

Before arriving at the haunted location, try to determine the kind of ghost you are investigating in order to best plan an appropriate procedure.

If there is a pattern to the haunting, it is probably an imprint ghost and you will want to make the place where the ghost has observed in the past the center of your investigation.

If the ghost has been observed at more than one location, it is probably what is often termed a "haunting ghost" and you and your assistants will need to "stake out" as many locations as possible where it might appear.

If it is a poltergeist, you will want to draw a chalk circle around objects which have moved in the past and station yourself in the place where most of the previous activity has occurred.

Sometimes, a thorough preliminary investigation will reveal that the explanation for the haunting lies somewhere other than in the "haunted" location.

Andrew Green, in his excellent, *Ghost Hunting: A Practical Guide*, wrote of a case which, at first, appeared to be a classic haunting but turned out to be something else entirely. Upon purchasing a bakery in Sussex, England, the new proprietor "felt the presence of someone in the bakery." More than once she felt the unseen entity "push past her." Doors opened by themselves and her baking paraphernalia moved about the bakery. It was not long before her husband and son experienced the unexplainable phenomena as well.

When Green questioned the family who had owned and run the bakery for several generations, they stoutly declared that they had never experienced anything supernatural during their time there.

As he interviewed the family members, Green noticed that an elderly member of the family said almost nothing and he "seemed half asleep."One day the old gentleman died and all of the paranormal activity in the bakery ceased on that very same day, never to return.

Green deduced that the elderly baker, now retired and with nothing to occupy his mind, must have spent his days remembering his time as a baker and replaying in his mind all of the actions of his daily routine with such intensity that he, somehow, projected his presence back into the bakery and, caused the apparatus he had used in those days to move about in concert with his thoughts.

Search for a "Natural" Explanation

Try to find any "natural" explanation for the ghost-like phenomena which has been alleged to have occurred. Eliminate any preconceived ideas you might have. It is crucial that you keep an open mind and question everything.

Could frightening howls in the night be merely an owl or the wind rushing through trees or past some other object?

Could it be that objects said to move about turn out to move only when a heavy truck goes by?

Could a mysterious tapping sound be caused by birds, insects or tree branches brushing against a windowpane?

One of my favorite examples of less than supernatural phenomena involved a piano from which otherworldly sounds often emanated. When the piano was examined closely, it turned out that mice were contentedly chewing away on instrument's felt pads!

Preliminary Procedures
for
Detecting Hoaxers and Unforeseen Intruders

Once you have determined that no natural explanation can be found to explain the alleged paranormal phenomena and you have set up any equipment you may wish to deploy, your next task is, if possible, to seal off the area which is thought to be haunted as best you can in such a way as to detect any animal or living person who might, for any reason, enter the area.

Doorways may be unobtrusively "sealed" by stretching a piece of fine thread across the opening of the passageway and firmly securing both ends of the thread to the doorframe with museum putty or some other nondestructive adhesive. Should anyone pass through the doorway, they will either break the thread or pull it from the adhesive on one side of the doorframe. It is vital that the thread be thin enough to easily break when someone passes through it in order that any physical intruder could not possibly be injured.

You can use this same technique to test the nonphysical nature of ghost, as Rosina Despard did in the case of the Cheltenham haunting, by stretching the thread across an area through which the ghost is said to often pass. If you are fortunate enough to see an apparition and it passes through the thread without breaking it, you will know that it was, indeed, a ghost and not a hoaxer masquerading as a phantom.

Another more foolproof method of constructing a seal on a closed door is to write your name on a very thin and narrow strip of paper. Adhere with a nondestructive adhesive one end of the paper to the edge of the door close to the doorframe near the top of the door (so that anyone entering the doorway will not be likely to see it) and adhere the other end to the door frame. Should anyone open the door, the paper strip will be torn. As you have written your name on the strip of paper, should a hoaxer see the paper fall to the floor after opening the door, he will be unable to duplicate your signature in an attempt to replace the broken seal with any duplicate he might attempt to make.

Another way to "catch" an intruder or someone who inadvertently enters the area is to spread a thin layer of flour and sugar onto the floor. Should anyone other than a ghost cross the floor, he will leave footprints and, if he is nearby, you will likely hear a crunching sound as he walks upon the sugar.

If you have taken these precautions and something moves within the sealed off area, you can be certain that it was not intentionally moved by someone perpetrating a hoax or by someone who has inadvertently wandered into the area and moved the object.

I wish I had used this technique many years ago when I investigated a well-known haunting at the historic Robert Louis Stevenson House in Monterey, California. Shortly before closing time I had placed an antique book on a bed and another antique book on the floor in one of the rooms which was furnished as it might have looked when, in 1879, the then unknown Robert Louis Stevenson lived in the house for a short period of time.

A California State Park ranger locked up the house a few minutes after I had positioned the books and the property was now secure. As the ghost believed to haunt the house was said to occasionally remove books from a bookshelf, I was hoping that, in the middle of the night, she might prove her presence by moving one of the books I had placed in the room.

The next morning I arrived at the Stevenson House a few minutes before the ranger arrived and unlocked the door. When I made my way upstairs, I found that both books had been moved from where I had left them and they were now neatly stacked one upon the other. I felt certain I had obtained proof of ghostly activity. Unfortunately, I later learned that a custodian had come in to do some cleaning in the middle of the night and he had moved the books.

A simple piece of thread stretched across the room's doorway which I would have seen to have been broken when I checked the room the next morning would have saved me a considerable amount of embarrassment.

The Ghost Watch

Once you have made all of the necessary preparations, you will be ready to wait and watch for the appearance of an apparition, phantom noises or poltergeist activity.

Unfortunately, the sad fact is that, more often than not, you will find yourself patiently waiting for hours for something dramatic to happen only to find that that nothing of a supernatural nature occurs. Ghosts are notoriously fickle entities, appearing to one person while remaining unseen by another, appearing to several people one day but not appearing again for months. Sometimes they remain inactive for decades only to unexpectedly reappear when renovations are made to the building in which they reside. Furthermore, the fact of a site once being haunted does not necessarily mean that it is still haunted today. While some ghosts seem to stay forever, others tend to fade away with time.

I once waited up all night peering into the haunted nursery of the Robert Louis Stevenson House hoping to see ghost of Manuela Giradin who, in December of 1879, had nursed her two grandchildren through a case of typhoid fever in that room, only to succumb to the fever herself on December 21st.

Although others have reported clearly seeing her, attired in black with a high lace collar, she did not appear for me that night. Nor did I see the rocking chair in the nursery rock gently back and forth or smell the odor of carbolic acid or the scent of roses or feel a ghostly hand upon my shoulder as others have reported. Neither did I see the little girl said to move toys about the room or see any of the toys move. I have no doubt that those who have observed these manifestations over the years were truthful in their reports. It is just that the conditions were not right that night for them to occur for me or, perhaps, I was not in the frame of mind necessary for me to observe them.

Likewise, although I felt the unshakable sense of someone watching me throughout the night I spent alone in the sixteenth century Ross Castle in County Meath, Ireland, I never experienced any substantial manifestations of either of the two ghosts said to haunt the castle.

When performing a solo play in the famously haunted Charleville Castle just outside Tullamore in County Offaly, Ireland, I was offered the unique opportunity to sleep for two nights in a room which was said to be particularly haunted. I was warned that the last two times anyone had been allowed to sleep in that room, in each case, the guest sleeping there had, in the middle of the night, seen something so frightening that he fled the room in terror. Unfortunately, I experienced nothing more than two delightfully comfortable nights sleeping in the most beautiful room I am ever likely to occupy.

And, yet, as the reader is already aware, I have, over the years, seen apparitions and heard phantom voices and other paranormal sounds when I least expected it. One never knows when the conditions will be right to experience the paranormal.

How Might a Ghost Appear?

If you are so fortunate as to see an apparition, how the ghost might appear can vary from person to person and from one occasion to the next. It all depends on several factors ranging from the state of mind of the person who sees the ghost at the moment it is encountered to the type of ghost one encounters.

A ghost might appear as anything from an indistinct body of light or shadow, to a transparent figure, to a figure so substantial that it might be mistaken for a living person. Furthermore, it is not at all unusual for one person to see a ghost quite clearly while those around him see nothing at all.

And, then, in the case of an imprint ghost, the appearance of the ghost could depend upon how long ago the ghost was created.

Andrew Green has theorized that a finite amount of energy is created when a ghostly image is imprinted into the place where it will, from time to time, be observed and that this energy dissipates over time, causing the appearance of the apparition to change over time as well.

In his book, *Ghost Hunting: A Practical Guide*, Green cites the example of a haunted mansion in which, in the 18th century, the apparition of a lady in a red gown, wearing red shoes and a black head-dress was, at times, observed in a particular hallway. Years later her gown and shoes were seen as pink by those who encountered her and her head-dress was described as being grey in color. In the mid-1800's she was referred to as "a lady in a white gown" with grey hair. Sometime before the Second World War, she had faded to the point that she was no longer visible and only "the sound of a woman walking along the corridor and the swish of her dress" remained of the ghost. Finally, just prior to the mansion being pulled down in 1971, workman reported feeling a mysterious "presence" in the hallway in which, years before, she had so often been seen.

If you do see an apparition or experience poltergeist activity it is important that you try to remain calm and attempt to observe as many details as you can of the event. Try not to move until the apparition is about to proceed beyond your range of vision or any poltergeist-like activity has ceased. Then record your observations, with as many details as possible, immediately while the event is still fresh in your mind.

Mediums and Psychics

Some paranormal investigators often include a medium or psychic as a part of their team. Whether they call themselves mediums, channelers, psychics or emphaths, these are individuals who profess either to be able to communicate with or to merely see ghosts. While some claim to be able to use their "gifts" while in a normal, waking state, others require going into a trance in which it is claimed that a departed spirit is able to speak through them or, in some cases, through an entity which they call their "spirit guide."

I, myself, many years ago, often attempted this approach using as my "medium" a hypnotized individual whose natural psychic abilities I had attempted to enhance through previous sessions of hypnosis. Unfortunately, neither I nor anyone else of whom I am aware has ever succeeded in obtaining specific information, of which the medium was not or could not have been previously aware, unmistakably proving the identity of a ghost in this manner. Mediums will often offer vague fragments of information such as "I see an unhappy man and the letter 'J' comes to mind," or, in some cases, a complete name with an entire biography. However, I am not aware of any medium bringing forth specific information, to which the medium could not have had prior knowledge, which was later be proven to be correct when checked again historical records.

I am not saying that all mediums are frauds. While many psychics and mediums *are* charlatans who prey upon those grieving the loss of a loved one, in my experience, most mediums are honest, caring individuals who have some degree of actual psychic ability but who are unable to produce meaningful results on demand and who are not always able to distinguish their true psychic experiences from those which are merely fantasies.

In particular, I would steer clear of professional psychics or mediums, especially those who appear on television or hold public demonstrations of their "abilities." There is nothing these shameless frauds are able to do which cannot be reproduced by magicians utilizing what is called the "cold reading" technique or other "tricks of the trade" known to members of the magic fraternity.

Sometimes the professional psychic will come up with such detailed and compelling information that it would appear to be proof positive of their ability to see and communicate beyond the grave. In these cases, however, they may have either planted an associate in the audience who plays the part of a complete stranger or an associate may have mingled amongst the crowd prior to their entering the theater in order to overhear conversations containing information which is passed on to the "psychic" prior to his performance or is transmitted to the "medium" during his performance via a radio channel into a tiny earpiece worn by the charlatan.

For decades a number of scientific organizations have offered large cash prizes to any psychic who can demonstrate his or her abilities under strict scientific controls. From 1965 to 2015, the magician, James Randi, known as "The Amazing Randi," offered a cash prize to anyone who could demonstrate supernatural or paranormal abilities under an agreed-upon set of scientific controls. While the prize was at first only a thousand dollars, it increased over the years to, in 1996, one million dollars. Although many attempted to win the prize, no one ever succeeded. As no high profile "psychic" ever dared having his or her abilities tested under Randi's conditions, in 2015 the offer of the million dollar prize was finally withdrawn.

I am not suggesting that psychic ability does not exist or that there are not individuals with extraordinary paranormal abilities. I am a firm believer in both. I have seen far too many examples of psychic ability in normal, everyday life to doubt it for an instant. What I am suggesting is that these abilities occur on a spontaneous basis and that these abilities cannot be called upon and demonstrated at will. I very much hope that I am wrong in this regard and that I will, someday, meet a psychic who can demonstrate his or her abilities at will and under tightly controlled conditions. But, so far, I have not encountered such an individual.

Another problem inherent in utilizing psychics in the investigation of a haunting is the problem of telepathy. Even if the medium or psychic is able to come up with verifiable information which he or she could not possibly have known, this would not be proof of the medium being in contact with a ghost if this information was known to anyone present at the investigation. If the information brought forth by the medium was known to anyone involved, it would be impossible to rule out the possibility of the medium having gained that information through telepathy. Although this would be impressive proof of the medium's psychic abilities, it would not be proof of the medium having communicated with a ghost.

Electronic Voice Phenomena

While waiting for an apparition to appear or for other paranormal events to occur, many investigators attempt to record electronic voice phenomena, often termed "EVPs."

One procedure is to let a recording device, either a magnetic tape recorder or a digital recorder, run for a long period of time in the hope that, upon playing it back later, a voice will be heard which was inaudible to the human ear but was, somehow, able to be recorded by the audio recorder.

Another method is to ask questions of the spirit presumed to be haunting the site, let the tape run for twenty seconds of so, and, then, play it back in the hope that a disembodied voice will be heard answering the investigator's question.

Recording EVPs has become extremely popular in the wake of the numerous "ghost buster" shows on television in which self-described paranormal investigators attempt to prove that a site is haunted through the use of pseudoscientific electronic devices such as electromagnet field detectors, thermographic cameras and infrared thermometers, none which, as discussed earlier, have been proven, in a scientific manner, to be able to indicate the presence of a ghost. As these shows never come up with anything which could be considered to be hard evidence for the ghost they are investigating and television producers need to end each episode with some kind of "proof" as to the existence of the ghost their team has been pursuing over the course of an hour, they usually resort to using EVPs as the "proof" presented at the end of the show.

The problems with EVPs, however, are many. First both magnetic tape recorders and modern digital recorders have been known to record otherwise inaudible radio signals and local landline telephone conversations. Unless the investigator is able to shield their equipment from all such interference, (something never attempted on these television shows,) there is no way to determine the source of the EVP.

Second EVPs are normally extremely short, lasting only a few seconds, and they are, almost always, so unintelligible that one has to listen to them over and over again, before one can make any sense out of what is being heard. At this point, what is called <u>apophenia</u>, "the tendency to perceive meaningful connections between unrelated things," comes into play. To put it the most simply, the human mind tries to find patterns in what we see and hear, such as seeing animals or faces in clouds or the amusing cases of the face of Jesus being seen on a piece of toast. The EVP might be considered the auditory equivalent of the famous Rorschach inkblot test in which the subject sees a pattern in what is a randomly created design.

In a study printed in the scientific journal, *Applied Cognitive Psychology*, researchers, Michael A. Nees and Charlotte Phillips, examined EVPs taken from the popular *Ghost Adventures* television show. Participants in the study heard the *Ghost Adventures* EVPs, recordings of actual human speech, recordings of actual speech obscured by noise and recordings of only noise. Among other finding, the researchers reported that only 13% of the participants in the study who said they heard a voice in the *Ghost Adventures* EVPs agreed on what the voice had said as opposed to 95% of the participants in the study who agreed on what they had heard when listening to what was actual speech. Even more damning was that the researchers found that their participant's interpretation of what was said in the *Ghost Adventures* EVPs agreed with what the television ghost hunters claimed was said less than 1% of the time.

This may explain why on these shows the EVP is usually played over and over again a number of times with the ghost hunter's interpretation displayed on the screen as the EVP is being played. It is only after reading the ghost hunter's interpretation of the EVP, while hearing the EVP, over and over again that the television viewer's mind is tricked accepting their interpretation of the EVP.

And then there is the obvious question which nobody ever asks. If a ghost is actually trying to communicate with the ghost hunter, why does it not do so in a voice that is so clear and unambiguous that its message cannot possibly be misinterpreted. In the few well-authenticated cases we have of ghosts speaking to those to whom they have appeared, there is never even the slightest question as to what the ghost has said.

While all of this suggests to me that EVPs are of little to no value, research into the subject still continues and it may be worth your time attempting to record them yourself in the hope of obtaining something meaningful or in making your own judgment as to their value. One of the exciting things about paranormal research is that new ways of exploring the unseen world are continually being developed.

Séances and Ouija Boards

While it may be tempting to try to make contact with the ghost you are investigating in the course of conducting the actual investigation through a nineteenth century style, table-tipping, spirit-rapping séance or via a Ouija board, I would strongly caution you against doing so. The point of your work should be to carefully examine every aspect of the alleged haunting under the strictest, the most controlled and the most objective set of conditions that you can devise. There are no controls or scientific safeguards when it comes to a séance or the operation of a Ouija board. Furthermore, it would be impossible to keep your eye on all of the objective aspects of the investigation while you are in the midst of an attempt to communicate with an unseen entity.

Still, should you be interested in exploring these techniques there are facts of which you should be aware.

The old-fashioned séance in which the participants sit around a table with their hands placed upon its surface, as in the "Phillip" experiment, calling out to any spirit present to move the table, depends upon what scientists call an "ideomotor effect," tiny imperceptible muscular contractions unconsciously produced by the participant's subconscious which cause the table first to slightly vibrate and, in some cases, to actually begin to move.

The Ouija board works via the same principle. When the operators of the board place their hands upon of the heart shaped planchette which then glides across the board, seemingly of its own accord, spelling out answers to their questions, the planchette is not being moved by a ghost. The movement is due to the operators' subconscious minds, working in conjunction with their eyes, controlling the planchette through involuntary muscle contractions. This has been proven by experiments in which the participants are asked to operate the Ouija board while blindfolded. Not being able to see the board, only meaningless strings of unrelated letters or numbers are spelled out by the planchette. Of course, if a spirit was directly controlling the planchette, there would be no need whatsoever for anyone to place their hand upon the planchette. It is reasonable to expect that the ghost would be able to move the planchette about the board all by itself.

The Pendulum

A pendulum is also sometimes employed by ghost hunters as a tool with which to communicate with ghosts. The pendulum is what is termed a "psionic" device. A light weight is suspended from a short length of a thin string, thread or a chain. Holding the end of the string in one hand, the operator asks for the pendulum to swing in the direction which will indicate the answer "Yes" to the operator's questions. Next the pendulum is asked to show in which directions the swing will indicate "No" or "Maybe." The operator is now ready to ask any question which could be answered by any of those three responses.

As with the Ouija board's planchette, the pendulum is controlled by imperceptible, unconscious muscular contractions which transfer energy down the string to the weight at the other end. Unlike the Ouija board, however, as only one person is controlling the pendulum and there are no visual cues to complete whatever psychic knowledge might be lying untapped within the operator's subconscious mind, the pendulum might, possibly, be a tool with the potential of transferring that knowledge from one's subconscious to one's conscious mind. That being the case, I feel that experimentation with a pendulum might be time worth spending.

Conclusion

I hope that, after, carefully evaluating the firsthand accounts presented within these pages that you, like me, will have come to the inescapable conclusion that, while we may not, yet, understand precisely what ghosts are or why they exist, that they and, perhaps, some other even more inexplicable entities, do, indeed, exist among us.

Should you decide that the subject is worthy of serious investigation, I hope that you might consider employing some of the procedures I have suggested in your investigations as well as original techniques which you, yourself, might invent along the way.

There is no need to purchase any of the, so far unproven, pseudoscientific electronic devices you may so often see utilized by self-appointed television "ghostbusters" or the ultra expensive and extremely complex equipment utilized by legitimate researchers from universities and such highly respected groups as the Society for Psychical Research. Researchers who are so fortunate as to have equipment costing thousands of dollars often end up with results which are no more impressive than those obtained by investigators working with a bare minimum of inexpensive tools. It is the ingenuity and the ever questioning mind of the researcher rather than the sophistication and the expense of his or her equipment which makes all of the difference.

It is important to remember that what well may be the best examination of a haunting on record was Rosina Despard's investigation of the ghost in her home in Cheltenham. With nothing more than an intelligent, open and enquiring mind, a few lengths of string and pellets of marine glue, the daring nineteen-year-old investigated and preserved for posterity the details of the haunting with a precision and an instinct for what was most important which has never been equaled.

The world of paranormal investigation is waiting for you. You need only to open the door and join the likes of Rosina Despard and so many others who have dared to question society's long-held beliefs and explore the world beyond our five senses.

Should you choose to open that door and pass over the threshold, I wish you the best of fortune and good hunting!

A Selected Reading List

Baldwin, Gay. *Ghosts of Knighton Gorges.* 2010

Bennett, Sir Ernest. *Apparitions and Haunted Houses: A Survey of Evidence.* Faber and Faber, 1939

Crow, Catherine. The Night Side of Nature; or, Ghosts and Ghost Seers. Palata Press, 2016

Darby, Mildred, Introduction by Mark Lyon. *Leap Castle The House of Horrors: The Most Haunted Castle in Ireland.* Windwhistle Press, 2019

Goss, Michael. *The Evidence for Phantom Hitch-Hikers: An Objective Survey of the Vanishing Passenger from Urban Myths to Actual Events.* Weiser Books, 2015

Green, Andrew. *Ghost Hunting: A practical Guide.* Arima Publishing, 2016

Green, Andrew. *Our Haunted Kingdom.* Fontana, 1974

Hopkins, R. Thurston. *Ghosts over England.* Meridian,1953

Jourdain, Eleanor and Charlotte Anne Moberly, Tony Walker Editor/Translator. *An Adventure: A True Story About Time Travel.* White Rabbit Press, 2014

Lamont, Mark. *The Mysterious Paths of Versailles: An Investigation of a Psychical Journey Back in Time.* 2021

Lyon, Mark. *Haunted Nevada City and Grass Valley.* Windwhistle Press, 2021

Mark Lyon, *San Francisco Ghosts.* Windwhistle Press, 2016

Mac Manus, D. A., *The Middle Kingdom: The Faerie World of Ireland.* Colin Smythe Ltd, 1979

MacKenzie, Andrew. *Hauntings and Apparitions.* Heinemann, 1982

MacKenzie, Andrew. *The Unexplained.* Arthur Baker, Ltd, 1966

Middleton, Jesse Adelaide. *Another Grey Ghost Book.* Windwhistle Press, 2016

Middleton, Jessie Adelaide. *The Grey Ghost Book.* Windwhistle Press, 2016
Middleton, Jesse Adelaide. *The White Ghost Book.* Windwhistle Press, 2016

Seymour, St. John D., and Harry L. Neligan, *True Irish Ghost Stories.* Fall River Press, 2010

Stevens, William Oliver. *Unbidden Guests: A book of Real Ghosts.* Dodd, Mead & Company, 1946

Underwood, Peter. *Gazetteer of British, Scottish &Irish Ghosts.* Bell, 1985

Underwood, Peter. *Ghosts and How to See Them.* Trafalgar Square Publishing, 1995

Underwood, Peter. *The Ghost Hunter's Guide.* Bradford Press, 1987

Mark Lyon

Called "a master storyteller" by the *Times Colonist* of Victoria, Canada; actor and playwright, Mark Lyon, has, for over twenty years, toured across North America and Ireland performing original one-man plays as well as having recounted true ghost stories on scores of television and radio programs. In 2012 Lyon was honored to perform his solo play, *Ghosties and Ghoulies and Long-Legged Beasties and Things that Go Bump in the Night* at Ireland's prestigious Listowel Writers Week Festival.

Lyon wrote and narrated *Phantoms of the Holbrooke*, a film docudrama concerning the ghosts said to haunt Grass Valley's Holbrooke Hotel and he is the author of *San Francisco Ghosts* and *Haunted Nevada City and Grass Valley*. In his podcast, *The Other Realm*, Lyon recounts true tales of ghosts and other supernatural encounters throughout the world.

Photograph Credits

The Raynham Hall Staircase Ghost
Courtesy of Raymond Lamont Brown

The Tulip Staircase Ghost
Courtesy of Mary Evans Picture Library/
Peter Underwood

The St. Mary the Virgin Church Ghost
Courtesy of Syndication International

The Holbrooke Hotel Ghost
Courtesy of Mary Moore